Rainer Zerbst

Gaudí

1852 - 1926
Antoni Gaudí i Cornet –
A Life Devoted to Architecture

Taschen

Front cover: Güell Park, tower-like section of the roof on the porter's lodge topped by a "toadstool".

Back cover: The Sagrada Familia, view of the eastern façade from the inside.

Frontispiece: Photograph of Antoni Gaudí, 1878.

This book could not have been written without the existence of its predecessors. In 1978 Rikuyo-sha published a two-volume work on the architecture of Gaudí: **Gaudí: Arte y Arquitectura.**
The text for that work was written by Professor Juan Bassegoda Nonell, holder of the Gaudí chair at the Universidad Politecnica de Cataluna. It contained drawings of drafts for some of Gaudí's work done by Hiroya Tanaka. This book contains a selection of these.
In 1984 the Fundacio Caixa de Pensions in Barcelona organised a large travelling exhibition which was accompanied by a catalogue. Professor Juan Bassegoda Nonell arranged and supervised the exhibition and wrote the text for the catalogue, which was translated into six languages. It contains a number of illustrations supplied by the photographers at the Fundacio Caixa de Pensions. The illustrations come from the archives of the Gaudí Chair at the Universidad Politecnica de Cataluna, the most distinguished institute in the field of research into Gaudí's work. Some pictures from the catalogue have been used in this book. The catalogue's comprehensive documentation was indispensable for the concept of this book.
In 1985 Rikuyo-sha published a one-volume edition of his 1978 Gaudí work entitled **Gaudí: Arte y Arquitectura,** which constitutes the basis of this book. The publishers would like to thank all those concerned for their preliminary work.

© for this edition 1991 Benedikt Taschen Verlag GmbH, Hohenzollernring 53, D-5000 Köln 1
© 1985 Rikuyo-sha Publishing, Inc., Tokyo, Japan
Photographer: François René Roland
English translation: Doris Jones and Jeremy Gaines
Printed in Spain
ISBN 3-8228-0074-0
GB

Table of Contents

Gaudí  — A Life Devoted to Architecture

Half of Barcelona, it is said, was in mourning on June 12, 1926. The funeral procession, which slowly wound its way from the Hospital de Santa Cruz in the old section of Barcelona to the church of the Sagrada Familia, was half a mile long. For two and a half miles, thousands of people lined the streets along the way to pay him their last respects: Antoni Gaudí i Cornet, the "most ingenious of all architects," as his friend and colleague Joaquim Torres García once said of him, the "most Catalonian of all Catalonians." And indeed, there was hardly a dignitary from his native region who was not among the mourners in the procession.

Gaudí had long held the status of a folk hero. The government instructed that he be laid to rest in the crypt of the as yet unfinished Sagrada Familia, and the Pope granted his approval. It was thus that Gaudí came to rest at the site to which he had devoted the last 43 years of his life; and for the last 12 years it was, in fact, the only site at which he worked. He had created his own homeland, and he was accorded a magnificent funeral.

Just five days before, however, things had looked completely different. He was taking one of his late-afternoon walks — as he did every day after work — to the St. Philipp Neri church to pray; on the way there, he was hit by a tram and dragged along the street behind it. Gaudí fell unconscious to the ground. No one, however, recognized the architect who, although already a famous figure in Barcelona, was hardly ever seen in public. Taxi drivers refused to transport the shabbily dressed man to the hospital (for which they were later severely punished). Passers-by then took pity on the critically injured man and tended to him. A peculiar end for one of Spain's most renowned architects. And yet this mixture of contradictions is characteristic of Gaudí's life. For, if Gaudí, in the end, was celebrated as an outstanding figure by the public and the government, and especially the people, this was not because of his humble origins, but in spite of them.

He was born in Reus on June 25, 1852 as the son of a coppersmith. In other words, he was not the product of a particularly affluent environment. Moreover, little Antoni was plagued by illness from an early age. Rheumatic ailments already prevented him as a child from romping around on the streets with others his own age. The boy was often obliged to stay in the house; sometimes he had to be carried by donkey. His whole life was marked by this affliction: he had to deal with bouts of rheumatism until he died. The doctors prescribed a strict vegetarian diet and regular exercise in moderation, which included his customary walks to the church of St. Philipp Neri. And even as a youth Gaudí went on long walks throughout the area — an unusual pastime in those days.

It is surely fruitless to speculate whether Gaudí would have still taken his place in Spain's history as the architect he proved to be without his illness. After all, even if little Antoni could not move about freely, he was at least able to give his eyes — and his thoughts — free rein. He must have been a precocious child who baffled his elders with his amazing insights. When a teacher once pointed out that birds can fly because they have wings, Antoni immediately retorted that chickens in the barnyard also have wings, but only use them to walk. He never lost this sharp eye for detail and the habit of learning from the everyday world around him; indeed, it left its mark on all of his works. His interest in architecture had, incidentally, already come to light when he was a schoolboy in Reus (the school has, of course, been named after him), and at the age of 17 he went to Barcelona to study architecture.

Above: A drawing of the house at 4, Calle de San Juan in Reus. It is thought that Gaudí was born there. The house is no longer standing.

Left: Gaudí in his study in the Sagrada Familia. The drawing was made by Ricardo Opisso.

Proyecto de un palio para esta Ex.ma D.on

Escala 1/5

Barcelona 6 Octubre 1876

8

Left: Gaudí's plan for the cemetery gate, submitted to the academy in 1875 for his examination in "Drafting".

A Genius or a Madman?

As a student he lost none of his practical-mindedness: in addition to pursuing his theoretical studies in seminars and at the drawing board, he worked – to earn money – in the offices of several local architects.

He does not seem to have been a particularly good student, but good enough to acquire solid training in the fundamental principles of architecture; his draft of the cemetery gate was marked as "outstanding" and enabled him to pass his examination – though apparently not without some difficulty. His time at the university was not only revealing in terms of his enthusiasm for architecture; it also showed his strong-minded temperament. In order to give his design-drawing more "atmosphere," he had started by drawing a hearse and, apparently, rendered a much more precise drawing of this carriage than of the subject matter at hand. The professors were not blind to Gaudí's talent for doing things his own way. There was no doubt in the mind of the chairman of the Faculty for Architecture that this student who had been allowed to pass the examination was either a genius or a madman – an opinion Gaudí was to encounter more than once in the course of his career. For, although he had completed his studies in the proper manner, he soon parted ways with the prevailing rules of architecture.

Gaudí also drew his inspiration from books. He was by no means a revolutionary at the outset of his career. However, the search for a style of his own began in what was an unusually favourable climate for this endeavour. All of European architecture was in flux and receptive to change. There were no fixed, binding norms. The science of history had become established in the 19th century; the previous centuries had become the subject of research in art as well and thus accessible to the young student. The result was an eclecticism which was overwhelming at times.

A number of fashionable trends also contributed to this development. Following the austere Age of Classicism, people were beginning to break out of the corse of strictly applied rules. Romanticism had preached the

Above: The University of Barcelona (main façade facing the Avenida Gran Via de les Corts Catalanes).

Page 8: Gaudí's project for the covered courtyard of the provincial administration building in Barcelona (watercolour detail)

Fuente para la plaza de Cataluña

Above: Draft of a fountain for the Plaça de Catalunya in Barcelona. This fountain, which was to be 120 feet high and occupy the entire square, was never built.

Page 11: Design-drawing of a boat dock, elevation and front view (top), elevation and side view (bottom). Gaudí was not awarded the special prize he had hoped to receive for this draft.

freedom of feelings and of the subject. This was manifested most clearly in the style of gardens at the time. The era of the symmetrical, neatly trimmed and structured French garden was followed by the blossoming of the English landscape garden. Natural herbage was the maxim. Soon gardens that grew wild were all the rage – or rather, they were planted to look as if they were wild.

This was accompanied by a veritable fad for the past, the Middle Ages, which not so very long ago had still been defamed as the "dark" ages by the proponents of 18th century Enlightenment. The Gothic style underwent a revival – although the term Gothic was applied to anything that bore even the faintest resemblance to the Middle Ages. Palaces were built in the old style, and sometimes even artificial "ruins" were put in the gardens. A strong aversion to rigidly straight lines became widespread, and ultimately gave rise to a mesh of various ornamental lines which became one of the most fundamental elements of Art Nouveau.

The Spanish art world was not immune to all this, although the Iberian peninsula, a world unto itself, had always remained somewhat detached from the major trends in Europe. Nevertheless, the writings of the English art theorist John Ruskin were enthusiastically devoured in Spain, and this did not fail to have an effect – even on Gaudí. "Ornament is the origin of architecture," as Ruskin put it in 1853. Three decades later Gaudí would

advocate the ornamental in much the same way, and in his own ardent manner. The large iron portals of the Güell Palace, which he designed in Barcelona at the end of the 1880's, could hardly come closer to Art Nouveau.

The Dandy

Gaudí also studied the Neo-Gothic style propagated above all by French architects. Viollet-le-Duc's book on French architecture from the 11th to the 13th centuries became something like a Bible for young architects, and Gaudí was no exception. He even travelled to Carcassone, where Viollet-le-Duc had restored the old section of the city. In fact, Gaudí studied the walls so intensively that one of the villagers in the neighbourhood took him for Viollet-le-Duc himself, and paid him his due respects.

The fact that Gaudí could be mistaken for such a prominent figure had to do with his bearing during his early years as a young architect. When one thinks of Gaudí as the shabbily dressed old man who did not necessarily

Gaudi as a young man in 1878. Gaudi did not like to be photographed; this photograph is thus a rarity and is one of the few remaining photographs of him today. It shows the open-minded, attractive young artist, predisposed to the titillations of social life, at the beginning of his career. (The photograph is in the Reus Municipal Museum).

shun publicity but certainly did not seek it either, and did his best to avoid any camera in sight – which is why there are almost no photographs of him – then the image of the young Gaudí provides a startling contrast indeed.

It is true that Gaudí was not exactly blessed with wealth; throughout his studies he lived in rather poor conditions and thus had to earn money on the side; yet, he had barely left university before he set out to make up for all the things he had had to forego in previous years, or so it would seem. He developed an unmistakable penchant for a fashionable appearance, for being a dandy – which, by the way, was perfectly in keeping with the times, in which writers such as Oscar Wilde proclaimed that external style and refined, meticulous dress were the highest ideal. But Gaudí was a magnificent and – for Spain – completely extraordinary phenomenon: a head of full, blond hair, deep blue eyes and stalwart build – features which made him stand out. He bought his hats at "Arnau", the foremost hatter's; the young architect's calling card (which is on display in the Reus museum today) was carefully designed, and he had his beard tinted with an elegant touch of grey by Audonard, the top hairdresser's. Shoes were the only items of clothing he preferred "second-hand." He did not like to wear new shoes because they were uncomfortable, so he had his brother "break them in" for him; practical-minded as he was, Gaudí could be found all around town. How different Gaudí looked as an old man, who at most only took meagre meals and usually got up hungry from the table.

In his heart Gaudí always remained true to his origins. He felt close to the common people. When, after the accident with the tram, people finally recognized who he was, they wanted to move him to a more comfortable room in the hospital, but he insisted: "My place is here among the poor." That certainly is not in keeping with the young Gaudí's preference for high society – though it was of course more a matter of rubbing elbows with the high society of the mind, i.e. the intellectuals and artists.

Above: Harbour and Barceloneta in 1872. The photo shows the rapidly expanding outskirts of the growing industrial city. Below: The Passeig de Gràcia in 1870.

Left: Corner of the Rambla and the Calle de Pelayo in Barcelona. This was the site of the Café Pelayo – a meeting place for intellectuals, often frequented by Gaudí as a student.

PARANINFO

sección trasversal escala 1:50

Project for the entrance examination: cross-section of the university lecture hall. This draft already reveals Gaudí's tendency to combine various architectural styles, lending the work a quality of its own: the dome in the middle contrasts with the austere lines of the rectangular façade. Gaudí created a synthesis by intimating a gabled roof on the top of the dome. This mixture of styles may have astounded Gaudí's teachers at the academy, but the project was only given a "pass" mark – the lowest possible mark given by the university.

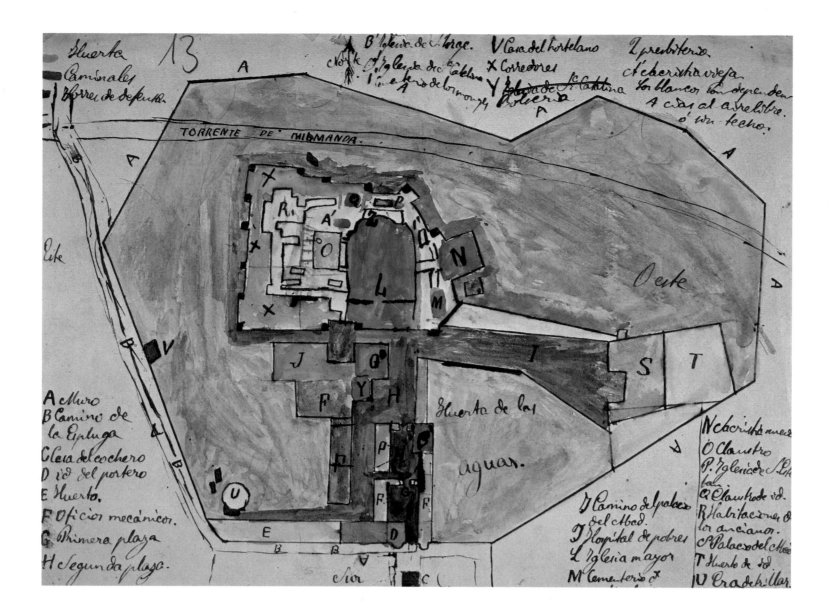

Draft of a plan to restore the cloisters in Poblet. This is one of the projects in which Gaudí participated while still doing coursework in preparation for his architectural studies.

Barcelona at the Turn of the Century

Barcelona was an enterprising city. The ancient walls had already been torn down in 1854, and the city was bursting on all sides. In the span of only a few years it grew in surface area from approx. 50 acres to more than 500. The population quadrupled during the second half of the 19th century. Thanks to the cotton and iron industries, trade flourished; the upper middle classes had never had it so good. Such developments raise the level of consciousness – in the arts as well. The rich liked to surround themselves with artists and writers.

It was not unusual for them all to live under the same roof. This, of course, was an ideal environment for an architect. It is not at all surprising, perhaps, that Gaudí designed nearly all of his buildings for Barcelona; he seldom had the need to look for other places to work. And this is why a Gaudí fan today need only take a walk through Barcelona to take in all of Gaudí's major works.

The aspiring architect's new social environment naturally affected his way of thinking. He soon adopted the anti-ecclesiastical attitudes of the day, popular especially among the young people. He was also fascinated by the new social theories and ideas. Although he felt at home in intellectual circles, he was also committed to the concerns of workers. It is surely no coincidence that his first major building project was devoted to providing accommodation for factory workers. It was based on collaboration with the Mataró workers' cooperative, an ambitious undertaking reminiscent of the ideas of Robert Owen, the English social reformer who, albeit an industrial magnate himself, zealously worked to improve the living conditions of workers.

The Mataró project was intended to create the architectural prerequisites for such an improvement. Apparently, however, the time was not ripe for such achievements: only a factory hall and a small kiosk were actually built, which somewhat disillusioned the young Gaudí.

Be that as it may, the Mataró project marked the beginning of what was to become growing fame. The project was exhibited at the Paris World Fair in 1878 and led to Gaudí's life-long friendship with Eusebi Güell, for whom he was to design numerous buildings.

However, that was still in the distant future. For the time being, Gaudí continued to search for his own style, allowing himself to be influenced by the prevailing trends – one of which in particular was Neo-Gothic. This, like the workers' project, was not entirely free of political overtones. While it is true that the rediscovery of the Gothic style was a widespread phenomenon of the day in Europe, it held a special attraction for Gaudí's home – Catalonia.

Even before he began studying architecture, Gaudí went on numerous hikes visiting the major works of architecture in the area. The dilapidated cloisters of Poblet was one of the sites which especially attracted him.

Gaudí – a Nationalist

Despite the economic boom in Catalonia, and although Catalonia could look back on a glorious past, the political situation of the region was deteriorating. Under Roman rule the country had rapidly grown into a trade centre, and in 343 A.D. Barcelona was declared a diocese in its own right. During the Middle Ages Catalonia – which was originally called "Gotalonia" after the Visigoths who made Barcelona the capital of their kingdom in the 5th century – was an autonomous county with its own laws and its own language. Modern times – and the emergence of the Spanish Empire under Castilian rule – saw the gradual loss of the region's independence; by the early 19th century, even use of the Catalonian language had been prohibited in the schools. Thus, for the Catalonians, the late 19th century revival of the Middle Ages, the discovery of the "Gothic" style, was more than merely a matter of artistic preferences: it became a political signal. Gaudí, too, was caught up in the wave of nationalist sentiment.

Gaudí became a member of the *Centre Excursionista,* a group of young men who made pilgrimages to the historical sites of the once glorious past. Gaudí considered himself a Catalonian through and through. He always insisted on speaking Catalonian, even when this meant that his instructions to the workers at the construction sites had to be translated. When, toward the end of his life, he once had to appear in court, he refused to answer in Castilian Spanish.

However, none of these political leanings made Gaudí a partisan to any political programme or party. His ties to the people and his homeland were of a more natural and emotional form. His trips to the monuments of the past, therefore, probably had no political significance for him. Rather, he used them to expand his knowledge of the great architectural works of his homeland. These included, in addition to the great Gothic cathedrals –

Sociedad cooperativa LA OBRE

Fachada al Jardin   Escala ⅟₅₀.

Draft plan for the refectory. Garden façade (left) and the façade on the street side (right) of the "Obrera Mataronense" (Mataró workers' cooperative). The plans for this workers' housing project date from the year 1873. At that time only the flag was designed; the various buildings were planned in 1878, but very few of them were actually built.

such as Tarragona, only some six miles from his native city of Reus — above all the Moorish structures of Spain's Arabic past. Again Gaudí found himself in good company, and in no small numbers at that. While once more lagging behind developments in the rest of Europe, Spain had also been marked by the widespread enthusiasm for the exotic. In central Europe this fashion of the day had already emerged in the 18th century once the threat of a Turkish invasion had passed — the Turks had been fought off successfully near Vienna in 1688, leaving behind no more than an attraction for what was foreign. The Moorish past had been a part of Spain's history for centuries, and thus the foreign and unusual held less attraction here. However, in the sweep of orientalism which prevailed in the upper-class salons of the 19th century, the fascination with the exotic began to take hold in Spain as well. The drawing that Gaudí submitted for the entrance examination at the university is already faintly reminiscent of Moorish façades, although it brings to mind the large domes of the Italian Renaissance.

MATARONENSE =Casino=

Fachada a la Calle

Initial Attempts

Gaudí never cared much for purity of style. He never made exact imitations, but preferred to draw inspiration from the buildings of the past. He thus kept completely to the teachings of Viollet-le-Duc, who had warned against the uncritical adoption of old models; as he saw it, the great works of the past were there to be analysed as a source of new insights which would help to create a style of architecture for the present. Gaudí's work seems to be the realization of this theoretical programme (and Viollet-le-Duc's "reconstruction" of the old section of Carcassone is in many respects also new and therefore more than a mere "reproduction"). The mixture of different architectural styles in the work Gaudí prepared for his entrance examination may have been the very reason why he was given only a "pass" mark, the lowest grade awarded by the university. The year before, a project that was similarly fantastic in nature had also failed to earn him the special prize he had hoped for.

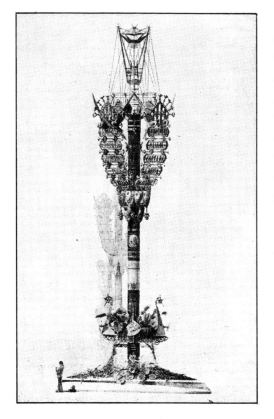

Above: Street-lamps designed by Gaudí for the promenade on the Passeig de Muralla del Mar in Barcelona. They reflect Gaudí's nationalist sentiments: the lamps were to bear the names of prominent Catalonian admirals.

Official recognition in the form of prizes was never forthcoming for the duration of Gaudí's life. Perhaps this is the reason why Gaudí always felt that he had failed in his work, or at least why he often made remarks to that effect. Apparently his architectonic ideas were too daring to win the acknowledgement and praise of the governmental or municipal authorities. Only once was he awarded a prize — and, as one might expect, for one of his most conventional works: the Casa Calvet. But then his work was seldom commissioned by "public authorities." Only at the beginning of his career did he have an opportunity to work for the city, a relatively small project: in February, 1878 the city of Barcelona commissioned the "young and industrious architect D. Antonio Gaudí" to design a street-lamp; the project was carried out, and well-received by both the press and the general public. Other than that, however, most of Gaudí's work was done at the desk and for the desk — plans, projects which, with few exceptions, never materialized; they included, among other things, a massive desk which looked like a small building that Gaudí designed for himself. However, the design has not survived.

Despite the lack of official public recognition for Gaudí, there was no lack of recognition for his work from other sources: private patrons who recognized his genius were always present in his life. After he had finished his first larger-scale projects, he was swamped with orders. Interestingly enough, he received his most important commission even before he had become known among the general public. He had not yet commenced

Right: Street-lamp on the Plaça Real in Barcelona. Designed by Gaudí.

In 1871 the Academy of Architecture in Barcelona purchased a number of photographs of Oriental buildings. The photographs fascinated the students and acquainted Gaudí for the first time with Oriental architecture in its pure form.

work on his first spectacular projects – the Casa Vincens, the country house El Capricho and especially the Güell Palace – when he was entrusted with the design of one of the most ambitious architectural undertakings in Barcelona. In 1881 the "Asociación Espiritual de Devotos de San José" (Association of the Worshipers of St. Joseph) had bought up a whole block of houses situated on what was then the city limits of Barcelona. A church for the adoration of the Holy Family (Sagrada Familia) was to be built on this piece of land.

The project was not free of political considerations. It was to be an expression of protest against increasing industrialization, against the loss of the old values. St. Joseph had been elevated in the 19th century to the status of the patron saint of those movements within the Catholic church which called for a reaction to its increasing secularization. The reference to the family was an appeal for a return to traditional values. In other words, the point was not merely to have a church building, but to surround the church with an entire complex of social facilities: schools, workshops, meeting rooms – a church-sponsored project on the same scale as that of the Mataró workers, on which Gaudí had worked so intensively shortly before.

However, nobody was thinking of Gaudí at this point; he was still too young and unknown. The architect Francisco de Paula de Villar, for whom the young Gaudí had already worked as a student – particularly on the Montserrat church – was commissioned to design the project. Villar submitted a model in the Neo-Gothic style and began with the excavation of the crypt. Subsequently, however, de Villar fell out with the Association and withdrew from the project. One can only speculate as to why Gaudí, of all people, was then entrusted with the responsible post. Perhaps it had something to do with his collaboration on the church in Montserrat, but also perhaps with the architect Juan Martorell. It was the latter who was first approached to continue with the work on the building, as he was, after

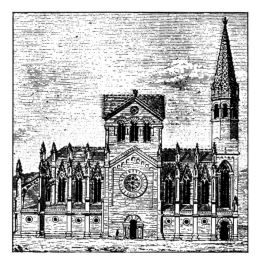

Above: Frontal view of the Sagrada Familia as designed by Francisco de Paula de Villar. The Neo-Gothic influence is unmistakable in the tall, straight pointed arches.

all, the leading representative of the Neo-Gothic style in Catalonia. However, Martorell declined. Gaudí had worked with him in the early 1880s, creating works composed entirely of a mixture of Neo-Gothic and elements of the Spanish ceramics tradition. Perhaps these samples of his work were the deciding factor: in any case, on November 3, 1883, Gaudí became Villar's successor and thus embarked on an architectural project which would occupy him for the rest of his life and to which he devoted himself exclusively in the last years of his life.

Up to this point, Gaudí had still had to prove himself as an architect. However, the order from the Association of the Worshipers of St. Joseph appears to have been the first step in what was to become a rising career. For, it was followed, in the very same year, by commissions for two major projects. Gaudí broke new ground in architecture with his very first work.

The brick manufacturer Manuel Vicens i Montaner had already taken Gaudí under contract to construct a residence in 1878. Work on the project began in 1883 in the Calle Sant Gervasi in Barcelona (today the Calle les Carolines). It is difficult to identify the elements of any particular style in this work, and any attempt to do so requires constant re-thinking. The building is not particularly original in terms of the ground-plan. Its appeal derives rather from the design of the outer façade and its interior. A Moorish influence is unmistakable. Small towers, reminiscent of the minarets on mosques, decorate the roof. Delicately fashioned tile patterns create the impression of the filigrain lattice patterns on Moorish buildings. The ornamental impression of the tiled walls is repeated in the interior. Yet this is not an imitation of Arabic architecture, which only served as a source of inspiration for Gaudí to create his own ornamentation. It would therefore be more appropriate to speak in terms of Mudejar rather than of a Moorish style. (Mudejar was a mixture of Spanish and Arabic architecture.) The smoking room comes closest to a purely Moorish style.

The "Moorish" Period

Below: The Plaza de Toros built by Emilio Rodriguez Ayuso in Madrid – an example of the Mudejar style of architecture popular at the time.

But the most intriguing aspect of this work is the mixture of materials Gaudí used in the building, combining unfinished rubble with ceramic tiles. This mixture of ornamental-looking tiles and cheap stone is a recurring feature in his work. And this, Gaudí's first great architectural achievement, is revealing of his style in still another respect: it took five years to complete. In other words, Gaudí's "organic" style of architecture, in which one idea leads to another, had already begun to evolve at this early date. Of course, the costs involved nearly drove Gaudí's sponsor to the brink of bankruptcy. However, he was richly compensated in the years to come: Gaudí's use of ceramic tiles initiated a veritable wave of fashion in Catalonia, and Vicens manufactured large quantities of these tiles.

Gaudí was engaged in construction work on a country house in Comillas, near Santander, at the same time as the Casa Vicens, and while the two are similar in style, the former was considerably more imaginative. Here, too, the foundations are made of undressed stone. But the walls are richly decorated with coloured tiles. The Moorish influence is even stronger in this work. A slender tower rises up like a minaret, with a "lid" on top – Gaudí's idea. But if one takes a closer look, one will see that it only appears to be Moorish and that the pattern of the tiles is totally European: a blossom that looks like a sunflower. This theme is a recurrent feature, and indeed its repetition also points to principles of Arabic architecture where repetition plays a predominant role. There is nothing uniform about this structure. It is thus deserving of its name: "El Capricho" - a caprice, a whim. It is not the only house designed by Gaudí that was given a nickname. People also liked to call the Casa Milà "La Pedrera" — the quarry — and not without reason.

For the time being, however, Gaudí's work was dominated by Moorish elements, although it cannot be said for certain, even in the case of an early work such as El Capricho, whether the tower is patterned after Arabic or Persian models.

While the projects in Comillas and Barcelona were still in progress, a strong friendship developed that was to influence his development as an architect for almost as long as his work on the Sagrada Familia in Barcelona. During the Paris World Fair, in which Gaudí's projects were also exhibited, he attracted the attention of a man whose personality was very similar to that of the young architect: Eusebi Güell i Bacigalupi.

The Casa Vicens, built by Gaudí between 1883 and 1888 in the Calle les Carolines in Barcelona. The contrastive use of tile ornamentation, above all on the corners and towers, is reminiscent of Moorish architecture, but Gaudí drew on his own imagination to design the tiles. The first of Gaudí's "Moorish works", it already reveals his highly individual approach to historical models.

The eastern façade of El Capricho. Gaudí worked on this manor-house for Don Máximo Díaz de Quijano from 1883 to 1885. Viewed from the east the house looks quite conventional; only the mixture of brick wall and green-yellow tile ornamentation alludes to the imaginative Mudejar architectural style on which the design of the front is based.

Güell – Gaudí's Great Patron

Güell was a typical representative of the new Catalonia. Brick-manufacturing had made him a wealthy man; travels to England had exposed him to new currents in art as well as to innovative ideas on social reform. It was not long before Gaudí became a welcome guest at the Güell house, where the doors were always open to artists. Perhaps it was in Güell's library that Gaudí first became familiar with the influential writings of William Ruskin and William Morris. In any case, he was exposed for the first time to preliminary forms of Art Nouveau during the evenings at the house, as poetry written by the Pre-Raphaelites, especially that of Dante Gabriel Rossetti, was often read on such occasions. This movement, both painters and poets, had advocated a return to the Middle Ages and aspired to freedom from the strict classicistic rules of art, especially through the use of rich ornamentation. In 1910, Güell was made a baron, but even before that, Gaudí saw him as the embodiment of nobility. Genuine nobility, as he once put it, is manifested in heightened sensitivity, immaculate conduct, and the proper social standing. He discovered all of these in Güell, who, for his part, had met his ideal in Gaudí: the combination of artistic genius and social commitment.

As early as 1883 Gaudí designed a hunting pavilion for Güell in Garraf that bore the same elements as the Casa Vicens and El Capricho — a combination of unfinished stone and tiles. It was never built. Then, in 1884, Gaudí redesigned Güell's estate in Barcelona. Here again, the Moorish influence can be encountered, with the standard miniature towers above the riding hall, for example. However, signs of new trends also appear. The garden-gate indicates that Gaudí had apparently already begun to incorporate elements of Art Nouveau from the north, and the interior of the horse-stables — now the location of the Gaudí professorship at the Technical College of Architecture — reveals those unmistakable Neo-Gothic elements that Gaudí would develop to perfection in the years to come.

Initial results of this new direction can be seen in his first major project for Güell. In 1886 Gaudí began with the manufacturer's large residential home in Barcelona, expanding it into a veritable palace. Here, Gaudí's eccentric style became manifest in full-fledged form. Instead of beginning with fixed plans for the building's construction, he worked on the design as he went along. Just as in nature, where plants undergo changes as they grow, so Gaudí's buildings, too, were the products of a gradual process. A small music room was originally to be set up on the periphery of the building for Güell, a lover of Wagner. However, this music room must have become so fascinating with each new phase of the construction process, that it was eventually moved back into the centre of the building until it spread out over more than three floors. The palace, which also has a kind of "underground car park" for horse carriages and a genuine "forest" of richly decorated, odd-looking chimneys, proved to be truly fantastic, a product of the imagination, despite the historical elements of style which always shine through: numerous metal Art Nouveau ornaments as well as pointed arches reminiscent of Gothic architecture.

The "Gothic" Period

The two other structures that originated in those years were much more austere, more "Gothic" in nature, and it is no coincidence that they served religious purposes. With respect to the school of the Order of St. Theresa in Barcelona, the Colegio Teresiano, Gaudí's task was confined to the upper floors, as the building was already under construction at the time. The building exhibits forms which are quite strict — one might say, Neo-Gothic in its purest form, albeit in Gaudí's special rendition. For, already as a student Gaudí had learned from his great model, Viollet-le-Duc, that the structures of the past could at best serve as sources of inspiration and should never be imitated. This corresponded entirely to Gaudí's own views; he found Gothic architecture fascinating, but also flawed, especially with regard to design.

Gaudí saw the flying buttresses — an indispensable component of Gothic architecture — purely as aids to bear the weight of the arches. He referred to them derisively as "crutches." He wanted to manage without crutches. The first indications of this are to be found in the soaring parabolic arches used in the upper halls of the Colegio Teresiano. By contrast, the massive façades of a residence Gaudí later designed in Léon, with rough walls interrupted by numerous pointed arched windows, looks like something taken from the Middle Ages, as does the large Bishop's Palace in Astorga.

Eusebi Güell i Bacigalupi, Gaudí's great friend and patron. As early as 1883, Gaudí designed a hunting pavilion for Güell near Sitges. This was followed by five further contracts. The photo shows the devout Catholic and cultivated industrialist in the year 1915, after having been made a baron.

The Bishop's Palace in Astorga (in León) is one of the works designed during Gaudí's second period. Neo-Gothic elements are recognizable, but Gaudí avoided drawing too closely on historical models.

The Colegio Teresiano, middle portal on the ground floor. It is here that Gaudí's parabolic arch design was perfected.

However, the design of the Colegio Teresiano already alludes to the element that Gaudí devised to overcome the "flaws" of Gothic design, i.e. the slanted pillars.

This endeavour took up all of Gaudí's energy, particularly as he was then proceeding with work on the Sagrada Familia – a task which he did in his spare time, as it were. There was hardly time for private life. He never married, although he was on the verge of doing so at least twice in his life. He later claimed that he had never felt the urge to marry. However, had the young American woman whom he happened to meet on one of his excursions to look at cathedrals not already been engaged, perhaps Gaudí would not have remained a bachelor. It is said that she preoccupied his thoughts for years after their meeting. At the age of 32 – or so it is said – he even went so far as to become engaged, although this is based on hearsay. In any case, one senses here the extent to which Gaudí lived for his architecture. He would have found little time for private matters.

The Road to a Style of His Own

After this brief interlude of works during which Gaudí followed a strict, more or less Gothic style, he immersed himself completely in developing his own style. Apart from the occasional reference to Art Nouveau, all imitative elements gradually disappeared from his work. This may be the most distinctive and possibly the only outstanding aspect of the residence he constructed in 1898 for the heirs of Pere Màrtir Calvet in Barcelona – a house which marks the beginning of Gaudí's exclusive concentration on "his" city, on Barcelona. He had never travelled much anyway, except for a few study trips. Otherwise he concentrated his efforts on Santander, León (the Bishop's Palace in Astorga and the Casa de los Botines) and, of course, on Barcelona. The reconstruction of the Cathedral of Palma de Mallorca was a prominent exception, albeit an intriguing project. In this "major work" of Spanish Neo-Gothic architecture, Gaudí moved the choir stalls from the main nave to the altar. This enhanced the soaring effect of the Gothic interior – a task that must have been especially fascinating for Gaudí, who was so intensely preoccupied with the principles of Gothic architecture.

Gaudí had made a name for himself in designing churches; his students (who were also fervent admirers) spread the word. The Casa Calvet and Casa de los Botines had given him practise in constructing residences. Yet he still had another important new discovery to make. And again it was Eusebi Güell who provided him with the opportunity and helped him to obtain yet another contract.

Gaudí received nearly all of his commissions through private contacts. He would in all likelihood not have been awarded the contract to design the Bishop's Palace in Astorga if it had not been for the influence of Bishop Juan Bautista Grau, who had been in Tarragona before he was called to Astorga, and had known Gaudí for quite a long time; he, too, was a native of Reus. Grau died while the palace was still being constructed, and there were immediate differences of opinion between the architect and the episcopal administration. Gaudí withdrew from the project. His successor changed the building plans – and the structure collapsed several times as a result. Gaudí's designs did not lend themselves easily to change.

A Park in the English Style

Gaudí's sphere of influence was expanded by means of an ambitious, new project initiated by Güell. Güell had found himself quite taken by the gardens in England, and wanted to create something similar in Barcelona. Gaudí was to create a garden-city in complete harmony with the countryside. In the end, only two of the buildings originally planned for the project were actually made. Güell Park is one of Gaudí's numerous unfinished works.

But the park itself is more significant than the two villas that were built; it became an architectural work in its own right, and one of unusual daring. Above all, it is the first major work that fully and completely tranformed the imagination of Gaudí – now an architect in his mature period – into reality. Although the plans were incomparably more ambitious than one might guess when viewing the finished results, the latter demonstrate that Gaudí nevertheless burst the mould of all previous architectural practises. The structures – especially the huge terrace in the centre – are audacious in shape. The design of the surfaces and edges attests to a freedom which even today is hardly matched.

With this project, Gaudí for the first time put his comprehensive concept of the architect's profession into practice. Even the person whose theories he adhered to most, John Ruskin, had advocated that the architect present a synthesis of the arts; the architect had to be both painter and sculptor. Gaudí united all of this in one person. The endlessly long bench, decorated with ceramic tile fragments, which runs through the park in the form of a

The Güell Pavilions, ventilation towers on the roof of the porter's lodge. For the second work commissioned by Eusebi Güell, at the end of the 1880s, Gaudí developed a peculiar, imaginative and mature design for the air ducts in the roof required to ventilate the house. Gaudí turned the small ventilation towers into quasi-surrealistic sculptures or comical "little church spires."

snake, has the effect of a colourful painting by Joan Miró. Gaudí uses the ceramic fragments to construct an almost surrealistic painting, a three-dimensional painting in the very midst of the countryside, if you will. From thence on he knew no bounds. He unwaveringly gave his architectonic fantasies full rein; these are, after all, anything but pure figments of the imagination, based as they are on a strict constructional principle.

Although he then turned his attention to the design of two residential complexes, Gaudí nevertheless created something entirely new in this area. From 1904 to 1906 he designed a residence at 43, Passeig de Gràcia

Güell Park with a partial view of the main terrace – a meeting place – embedded in a park-scape full of lush vegetation.

in Barcelona that was completely innovative. Whereas Güell Park revealed the overflowing imagination of an architect quite drunk with colours, the Casa Batlló showed him to be an architect who was diverging ever further from architecture as an artificial creation of the human hand. The greenish-blue sheen of the façade evokes the surface of the sea, crowned with little peaks of foam. The window sills and frames seem to have been moulded out of clay. The façade – although tightly inserted between the two soberly designed houses on either side – has been set into motion. Everything seems to be welling up and then receding. The roof, with its multitude of chimneys, looks like a miniature version of Güell Park. Central heating was not common in Barcelona, as each room was usually heated individually; this gave Gaudí the opportunity to put an array of capricious chimneys atop the roofs.

Juan Bautista Grau i Vallespionós, Bishop of Astorga, born, like Gaudí, in Reus. He was one of Gaudí's major supporters and commissioned him, in the face of opposition from the episcopal administration, to design the new Bishop's Palace in Astorga. Grau had a great influence on Gaudí in his efforts to come to terms with the Christian religion and church liturgy.

The population was dumbfounded. They had never seen the likes of this before. The house defied any form of classification. The amazement was even greater in response to his second major project, at No. 92 in the same avenue. This was not merely another case of Gaudí designing a relatively small house wedged into a row of other houses, but a huge corner house. Unlike the Batlló house, the façade is totally devoid of colour. However, the bulging effect is more intense. The protruding rounded oriel windows cling to the façade like honeycombs. The building as a whole is a single mass of backward and forward movement. One is reminded of the cave dwellings cut into the sides of mountains by African tribes – or of the catacombs of St. Peter embedded into the Salzburg hill. The flowing movement continues into the interior. With this work Gaudí reached the pinnacle of his organic style of architecture: the building seems to have grown naturally, and it does not involve the customary use of bricks or carrying walls. The house is more like a huge sculpture than a house in the conventional sense of the word.

His Life's Work

If the public had been taken aback by the Casa Batlló – the Casa Milà caused an uproar. At a loss for words, all they could do, apparently, was resort to irony. Numerous parodies appeared in the newspapers; nicknames such as "the quarry," "the pâté," "the hornets' nest" replaced the serious-sounding name "Milà" (the client who commissioned the work, pere Milà i Camps).

In view of this seemingly inexhaustible store of architectural imagination, it should not be forgotten that Gaudí was unceasingly preoccupied with the Sagrada Familia project. It was still not completed when Gaudí died. However, Gaudí was fully aware of the significance of what he had set out to accomplish. He considered himself as being in the great tradition of Mediaeval cathedral architects.

A cathedral is not the work of a single architect, but of several generations. St. Joseph himself will complete it, Gaudí used to say, not only because the project was ambitious in scope, encompassing not merely a church, but a small community. It also had something to do with the founders' resolution, which required that the church be funded exclusively through donations and tithes – a church of the poor. It was not unusual for Gaudí himself to go around collecting money to continue the construction

The façade of the Passion in the Sagrada Familia. Gaudí did not even live to see work begun on this section of the building; construction of the façade started in 1952, and the towers were completed in 1978. The photo shows the tower shortly prior to completion.

A familiar view of the Sagrada Familia even today: finished sections of the structure standing alongside construction work which has just begun.

work. After 1914 he did not take on any new work, but devoted himself exclusively to work on the cathedral. He eventually took up quarters in the workshop on the building site. As was his custom, he always discussed the project with the workers. As a result, many changes were made over the years.

One could write a book about the Sagrada Familia's design. It is a synthesis of Gaudí's creative impulses. The overly high, parabolically shaped arches are repeated in the design of the gigantic, slender soaring towers. The bizarre spires of the four towers on the façade devoted to the Birth of Christ reveal the same use of loud colours characteristic of Güell Park. The church was supposed to be colourful in any case. Gaudí always said that nature is not monochromatic. Whenever someone praised the nice sandy brown of the undressed stones used in the façade, he retorted laconically, "It's going to be painted over."

Above all, Gaudí used this church to develop his theory of how the Gothic style could be perfected. There are no supporting pillars or flying buttresses. His design concept of the slanted pillars stood the test of time. He had used these pillars most effectively in a crypt he designed for his friend Güell, who required it for his workers' settlement on the outskirts of Barcelona.

When Gaudí died so tragically in 1926, he left behind an unfinished opus. Perhaps this is in keeping with the spirit of his architecture, which worked less with fixed structures, but was increasingly patterned after nature. Gaudí did not bequeath us a polished theory, but only insights, which, however, go further than many a well-built model. He had no successors. His work could not be carried on. Whenever other architects assumed work on projects he had already begun, they betrayed Gaudí's original intentions, and as a result, the buildings he had so carefully designed did not last for very long. The Bishop's Palace in Astorga collapsed several times, whereas the vaulted wood construction of Gaudí's first major project — the factory hall of Mataró — has stood the test of time.

An Architectural Genius

It is difficult to speculate as to all the things that Gaudí could have done had he had modern materials such as reinforced concrete. On the other hand, he might even have rejected them. He refrained for the most part from using cement, for example, even though this construction material would certainly have been available to him. He preferred to build his pillars out of bricks. While his structures may appear rather extravagant, and the surface may look expensive as it shines in the sunlight from the south — Gaudí preferred to use everyday materials, and always went back to the great craftsman's tradition of his hometown: ceramics and smithery.

He created veritable wonders out of the simplest materials. Perhaps nature served as his model here, as it did in so many other ways. He departed ever further from the artificiality of building, coming ever closer to nature. "Do you want to know where I found my model?", he once asked a visitor to his workshop. "An upright tree; it bears its branches and these, in turn, their twigs, and these, in turn, the leaves. And every individual part has been growing harmoniously, magnificently, ever since God the artist created it." In the nave of the Sagrada Familia, Gaudí

designed a veritable forest of pillars which branch out and upward in many directions.

When Albert Schweitzer visited the church, Gaudí explained his approach by referring to the tired, plodding donkey who brings the Holy Family to Egypt: "When it became known that I was looking for a donkey as a model for the flight to Egypt, they brought me the most beautiful donkey in Barcelona. But I couldn't use it." He finally found the donkey he was looking for hitched to the wagon of a woman selling scouring sand. "Its head was hanging down, almost touching the ground. With a great deal of effort I was able to persuade the woman to bring it to me. Then, after the donkey had been covered, section by section, with plaster, she wept because she thought that it would not survive. That was the donkey for the flight to Egypt, and it makes an impression on you because it is not invented, but real."

It is this affinity with nature that also ultimately distinguishes Gaudí from the Art Nouveau artists with whom people like to associate him. The ornamental strain in Art Nouveau is based on natural forms, but remains purely ornamental, and above all two-dimensional, purely linear. For Gaudí, however, nature consisted of forces that work beneath the surface, which was merely an expression of these inner forces. For example, he studied how stone blocks behaved when placed under great pressure by putting them in a hydraulic press: the stones did not burst or fissure from top to bottom, but expanded in the middle — a phenomenon which, as Gaudí believed, had already been recognized by the Greeks, who made their pillars a bit stronger in the middle than at the ends.

Sagrada Familia, overall views of the cathedral. Left, Gaudí's sketch, which only conveys the atmosphere of the planned work. Right, the first published full view of the church based on a 1906 drawing by Joan Rubió i Bellver. Rubió was one of the architects with whom Gaudí liked to work.

Gaudí was a pragmatist. Unlike other architects of his time, he did not work at a drawing board. He was always present at the construction site, talking things over with the workers, thinking things over, making a draft, rejecting an idea. His drawings look like impressionist sketches, and not at all like design drawings.

Gaudí experimented before he built. In preparing the daring arch designs in the Güell Colony church, he devised a model out of strings, from which he suspended small sacks of sand, corresponding to the weight which the supporting arches and pillars would have to carry. This served as an "upside-down" model of sorts: a picture of it had only to be turned upside-down to get a clear idea of what the final structure would look like. This procedure is not at all uncommon today, decades after this first experiment. The workers often asked how something was going to hold up; but it did. Looking at the dressing table designed by Gaudí for the Güell Palace, one is prompted to ask the same question.

Gaudí's works could never have been designed solely on the drawing board. This was not only because of the organic-looking spatial design, but also Gaudí's specific feel for space. Gaudí's aspiration was to depart from conventional walls. His ideal of a house was an organic body that seemed to live in and of itself. He always went back to his origins, to the profession of his ancestors in his spatial designs. A smith was a man who could create a body from sheet metal. This called for imagination. Before he could begin working, the smith had to imagine a hollow space. Gaudí's best structures are such hollow spaces. This approach was so different to that of, say, Mies van der Rohe, who worked with clearly defined surfaces and walls as basic elements. It is characteristic that van der Rohe's father was a stone mason, a man, in other words, who did not create a hollow body out of flat material, but instead took something away, broke something off a solid body.

Gaudí's pragmatic approach also had its disadvantages, of course. He was not a theoretician; above all, he did not create a school in the strict sense. And, with the exception of a few works from his early years, he left no written documents. Most quotations attributed to Gaudí are based on hearsay. Moreover, soon after his death, Gaudí's style receded into the background of discussion. Bauhaus, with its functionally oriented style, set the tone of the day, and its fundamental features contradicted those of Gaudí's.

Architecture of the Future

There was, of course, no doubt in Gaudí's mind that his architecture would have implications for the future. When asked whether the Sagrada Familia was one of the great cathedrals, he replied: "No, it is the first in an entirely new series." However, this prophecy has yet to be fulfilled. But even though Gaudí's influence waned during the first half of the twentieth century, his significance for the Catalonian movement remained unchanged. When, in 1925, a scholar questioned the significance of Gaudí the architect, he unleashed a storm of protest and a heated debate which raged in the press for four months.

It would seem particularly suitable, considering the times in which we live today, to contemplate intensively the essence of Gaudí's architecture..

Two examples of Gaudí's principle of using forms patterned after nature. Above, the crests of walls in Güell Park, which seem to anticipate the palm branches above them. Below, the bell towers of the Sagrada Familia, shaped very much like seashells.

Page 32: Bell towers of the Sagrada Familia with the inevitable construction crane as an "added ingredient."

Photo of the model Gaudí used in order to experiment with the pillar design of the church.

Our situation is not so very different from that of 100 years ago, when Gaudí developed his art. We, too, have turned away from the grey façades, the all too clear-cut, sober lines. Although we have not as yet witnessed a direct and radical reaction comparable to that of Art Nouveau, Gaudí's comment on his Casa Batlló could almost be taken as a prophecy for the very near future: "The corners will vanish, and the material will reveal itself in the wealth of its astral curves; the sun will shine through all four sides, and it will be like a vision of paradise."

The voices heard today do not sound so very different. On the occasion of the international crafts trade fair held in Munich in 1974, Josef Wiedemann praised Gaudí's work with the following words: "His structures are soothing oases in the wasteland of functional buildings, precious gems in the uniform grey of the lines of houses, creations pulsating with melodic rhythm in the dead mass of their surroundings."

Gaudí's work remained but a torso. The Sagrada Familia is almost symbolic of this. It is more than just an example of Gaudí's magnificent

architectonic and religious vision – it transports his work as a phenomenon that continues to live and have an effect into our present. Even today, there is no way to predict when the cathedral will reach completion; work on the Western façade alone took thirty years. When Gaudí died, he left behind no more than the beginnings of an architectural work which existed rather more in his imagination than in reality. Shortly after Gaudí's death in July, 1926, Kenji Imai came from Japan to look at various underground stations in Europe. His impression of the Sagrada Familia reflects more the fragmentary status than the vision of a completed work: "The façade of the transept on the north-east side and the vaulting wall on the north-west side were finished, but not the dome. In other words, one could see up into the grey sky… The parabolic, 300-foot-high bell towers stood in pairs over the three gables as if they formed a cave of stalactites. The scaffolding reached up to the top of the towers. The word "Hosanna" was sculpted into the colossal stone, winding its way around the high towers…I took leave of the temple on that rainy day with a very heavy heart…"

The First Glorious Secret of the Rosary in Montserrat: the resurrection of Christ. In 1891 Gaudí was awarded the privileged commission to create this group sculpture for the Lliga Espiritual de Nostra Dona de Montserrat. The work is not one of Gaudí's major artistic creations, but it reveals his growing enthusiasm for religion as well as his nationalistic sentiment: the national colours of Catalonia can be seen above the group sculpture. His design of the Jesus sculpture met with protest, and Gaudí withdrew – as he so often did – from the project.

Casa Vicens

1883–1888

One can hardly imagine a more extravagant debut
for a young architect. It rises before one like a
fairytale castle from the Arabian Nights at 24, Calle
les Carolines in Barcelona. And yet, in reality, it is
quite a small house, and not even the home of a
prince, but the residence of a brick and tile
manufacturer. Ten years passed between the
building being contracted and its completion. But
proper work was done on it for only five years –
surely not a long time in view of the result. It unites
the Spanish bourgeois tradition (which it achieved
with amazingly cheap stone) and the centuries-old
Arabic tradition. Gaudí made something quite
unique out of the building, beginning in a more or
less Spanish vein at the bottom and becoming
increasingly Arabic towards the top, perhaps even
Persian – it is difficult to distinguish between the two.

Above: Balcony of a turret (left). One of the crowning bosses to the turrets on the roof (right).

Page 37: View from the Calle de Carolines onto the façade facing the garden (left) and the front facing the street.

When the brick and tile manufacturer Manuel Vicens commissioned Gaudí to design a summer residence in 1878, the young architect was almost totally inexperienced. He had only recently been certified as an architect, on March 15. By the time Gaudí actually began to work on the structure in 1883, in other words with quite some delay, he had only worked on publicly-funded buildings. Designing a residence was new territory for him. Moreover, the task was not exactly an easy one. The house had to be built on a plot of land which was not particularly large, and was set in a row of rather conventional-looking buildings.

In terms of its architectonic structure, this Gaudí residence is not very striking, either. Compared with the complex spatial structures characteristic of his later works, this house would even seem dull. The two storeys are divided up fairly equally, owing to the continuous line of the main walls. The foundation is more or less rectangular; only toward the entrance, to which Gaudí added a little atrium, does the dining room stand out a bit. And yet the Casa Vicens already attested to Gaudí's talent as an architect who combined imagination with originality. Above all, it is an early example of Gaudí's practical bent despite all his predisposition for the bizarre. For example, he situated the building at the very rear of the site, leaving the garden in one piece, making it seem much larger than it actually was.

The rectangular form of the foundation is thus already somewhat disguised. The extravagant decoration of the plain façade with numerous little protruding gables and the design of the outer surface of the walls provide an added touch. These walls look like small gems, although Gaudí used quite simple materials. The basis is an undressed ochre-coloured stone – of the sort Gaudí frequently used in later works – combined with rough bricks. This contrast is of itself intriguing. His rather ordinary brickwork dons the appearance – when set against the roughly chiselled undressed stone – of decorative stone. However, the outside of this house draws its fascination from the lavish use of coloured ceramic tiles which, on the one hand, seem to run like supports through the walls, and on the other, are arranged in the form of a chessboard pattern. These geometric ornaments, when viewed from a distance, are reminiscent of Arabic structures, although it must be said that one cannot yet precisely discern from this early work whether or not the pattern might be Persian. Here Gaudí was already playing with ornaments. Upon closer examination one can also make out indigenous elements: numerous tiles are painted with the luminescent orange tagetes blossoms that were growing all over the garden. And the small towers decorating the roof vaguely remind us of Moorish structures. Designed by Gaudí, the cast-iron gate that leads to the garden, with the fingered palm leaf as its basic element, is more reminiscent of Art Nouveau. The Casa Vicens is a collage of highly varied styles. If this house has one distinguishing characteristic, then if anything it is that of an inconsistent style. How else should one interpret the peculiar small figures sitting like cherubs on the edge of a small balcony? The Casa Vicens is an example of how, by means of pure surface design and an overly-abundant ornamentation, a sober building can be transformed into a little castle.

Page 40: Entrance on the south-west façade. The outside wall is made of rough undressed stone and decorated with tiles. Gaudí himself designed the pattern.

Page 41: Dining-room fire-place. The walls are covered with pictures of birds and branches.

Below: Gaudi alternated the chessboard-like pattern of blue-green and white tiles with colourful tile sequences with a recurring pattern of several tagetes blossoms.

Above: Ceiling of the gallery adjacent to the dining-room.

Page 42: Dining-room. The furniture also has the function of framing the walls. Reliefs of fruit in lavish abundance fill the spaces between the beams on the ceiling. The small remaining wall space is decorated with flower-and-leaf patterns.

Page 43: Smoking lounge. Stalactite formations hang from the ceiling as if in a cave. A coloured relief made of pressed board covers the upper portion of the walls. Blue and gold decorative tiles cover the lower portions of the walls.

Page 46: Dining-room ceiling. The stucco between the wooden beams depicts cherries and cherry branches.

Page 47: The ceiling of the small room on the first floor is meant to create the illusion of a dome.

The attractiveness of the ornaments continues inside the house. Here we also find a surprising mixture of styles which nevertheless creates the impression of stylistic purity – though only briefly.

On closer inspection of the details, the observer soon discovers that this is not the case. Thus, the smoking room may come closest to resembling a small Arabian cabinet. There is a water-pipe in the middle of the room; lavishly upholstered chairs and divans are grouped around it. But here, as in the case of the outer walls, there are tiles with realistic flower patterns, and the stalactite grapes hanging from the ceiling are certainly not of Arabic origin.

The dining-room – the most lavishly decorated room of the whole house – is most characterized by Art Nouveau. Precious stucco work with cherry branch patterns fill the space between the large wooden ceiling beams. The walls – kept in a warm brown tone – are decorated with vines of ivy, and the door frames are painted with bird motifs.

Gaudí's imagination seems to have known no bounds. He playfully made use of the widest variety of forms – the main thing was that they should look ornamental. There was even a pseudo-cupola which had been common since the Baroque period and which was achieved through careful manipulation of perspective. It is, however, brilliantly executed. For a moment one actually thinks one is looking up into the sky, seeing birds alight and taking flight. It is only at second glance that one recognizes the true character of this ceiling design.

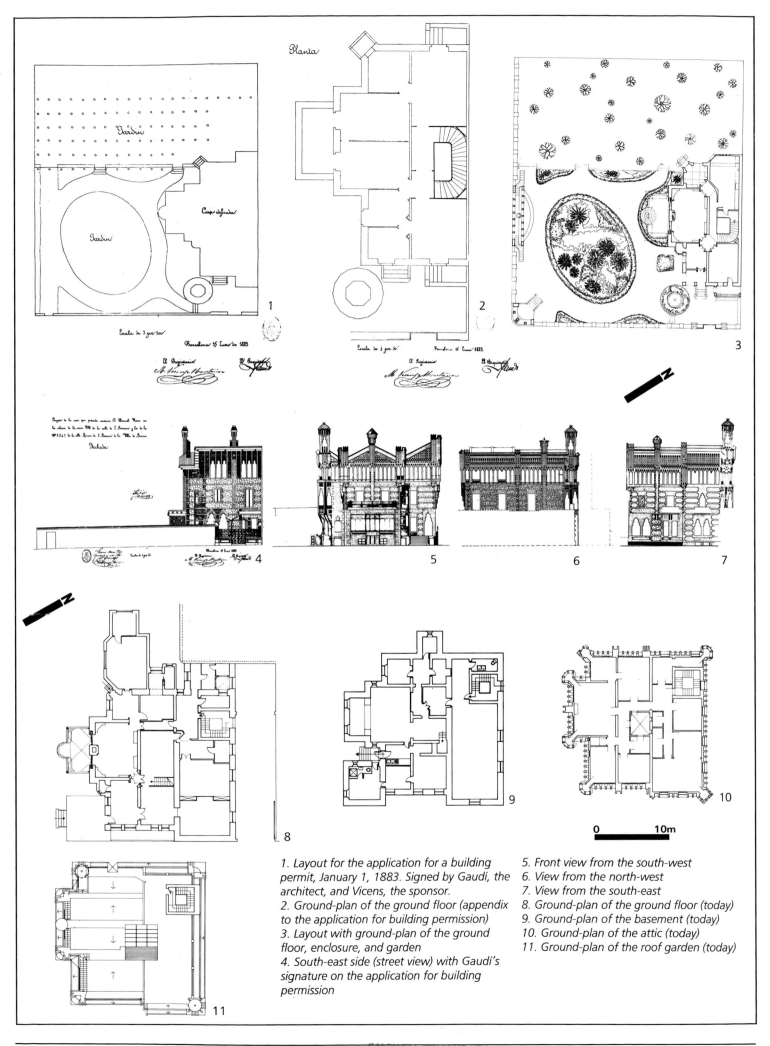

1. Layout for the application for a building permit, January 1, 1883. Signed by Gaudí, the architect, and Vicens, the sponsor.
2. Ground-plan of the ground floor (appendix to the application for building permission)
3. Layout with ground-plan of the ground floor, enclosure, and garden
4. South-east side (street view) with Gaudí's signature on the application for building permission

5. Front view from the south-west
6. View from the north-west
7. View from the south-east
8. Ground-plan of the ground floor (today)
9. Ground-plan of the basement (today)
10. Ground-plan of the attic (today)
11. Ground-plan of the roof garden (today)

Casa El Capricho
1883 – 1885

No one today will remember how this little house
came to be called *El Capricho*— a mood, a caprice,
perhaps also a whim. If it has anything to do with
the playful impression created by the house, then
it is deserving of its name. There it stands, as if it
had dropped from the sky, from another world,
and landed in the middle of a small green plot of
land in Comillas near Santander. It is Gaudí's
attempt to combine the Middle Ages, the golden
age of Catalonia, with the grace and dignity of
Oriental residences. It looks cumbersome: a
compact building with an evenly distributed tile
pattern embedded in the brick walls.
Even the tower, on its thick pillars, harks back to
the Dark Ages. But then the slender, richly
decorated tower rises cheekily like an inquisitive
finger pointing into the air, and the little roof
perched on top seems determined to defy all the
laws of gravity.

Page 49: The El Capricho manor-house ("The Caprice"), which Gaudí designed for a wealthy bachelor, stands on a plot in the middle of greenery.

Page 51: Steps lead up to the columned porticus on three sides. In keeping with his free use of styles, Gaudí employed variations on Attic columns. The rounded arches rising from the columns have a peculiar shape.

Actually, *El Capricho* would in fact have been an equally fitting nickname for the Casa Vicens. Both houses are colourful, resemble Moorish architecture, and were erected at about the same time. This may explain why, strictly speaking, these are twin buildings. The vaults and oriels – a constant source of surprise – and the variety of little towers on the Casa Vicens' roof make for a much more capricious impression than the manor-house built for Don Máximo Díaz de Quijano in Comillas, a small town near Santander. Here, too, the plot of land is not exactly large, yet the house stands, like an island, in the midst of its green surroundings. With this project Gaudí again achieved the impression of a Moorish-Oriental style through the use of tiles with Spanish flower patterns. Instead of the tagetes employed for the Casa Vicens, he chose blossoms resembling sunflowers. The ornamentation of El Capricho is, however, much more subdued, less imaginative, and less colourful. The main body of the building is comprised of nine alternating rows of bricks and flowered tiles, creating a very calm rhythm.

However, "moody" (another meaning of "Capricho") is a fitting description for the minaret-like tower as it soars straight upwards; it is solely decorative with no function whatsoever for the actual house. "Mood" could also be used to characterize the peculiar little balconies protruding at the corners of the house, and for which Gaudí contrived an over-sized trellis and "roof" made of thick, square iron bars. Although they appear to serve no purpose whatsoever, Gaudí used them to conceal a little surprise: he attached the counterweights for the sliding windows to two iron pipes in the trellis, so that when the windows are opened or closed the pipes begin to vibrate and produce strange sounds.

However, although the ornamentation of the façade seems somewhat staid by comparison with the colourful Casa Vicens – the architectonic

Below: This construction drawing shows the front view of the house (north side). At right, the sunflower motif on the coloured tiles which is repeated throughout the whole façade.

Hiroya Tanaka

structure of this, a bachelor's manor-house, is freer and more playful than it is in the latter. As soon as we approach the entrance, we notice one of the "moods" of this house. The view of the door is almost completely blocked by four relatively thick pillars and their delicately designed capitals which give way to three somewhat clumsy-looking rounded arches. The tower then rises up from this porticus. Despite all this masterfully executed whimsicality, however, Gaudí's talent as a pragmatist also came into its own. The roof – a part of the building to which the architect always devoted special attention – is relatively sober in Gaudí's terms, and above all surprisingly straight. He was making allowances for the local climate with its higher-than-average rainfall.

The design of the rooms differs considerably from that of the Casa Vicens. It is completely tailored to the needs of a wealthy bachelor. Whereas the dining-room was the focus of the Casa Vicens – it was significantly larger than the other rooms – *El Capricho* is but a one-storey building and consists mainly of rooms for socializing purposes: several bedrooms and guest rooms, a lobby, and above all a huge salon with a very high ceiling. This salon – a kind of winter-garden – forms the core of the house; the other rooms are grouped around it like additional extras. The lighting also differs from that of the Casa Vicens. The Casa Vicens has relatively few windows for its size, but the rooms seem all the more cozy and warm because of it. *El Capricho,* on the other hand, is filled with light. The walls of the main salon are to a large extent made up of huge windows separated

Below: Dining-room ceiling.

Page 53 below: Wood and marble ceiling of the bathroom.

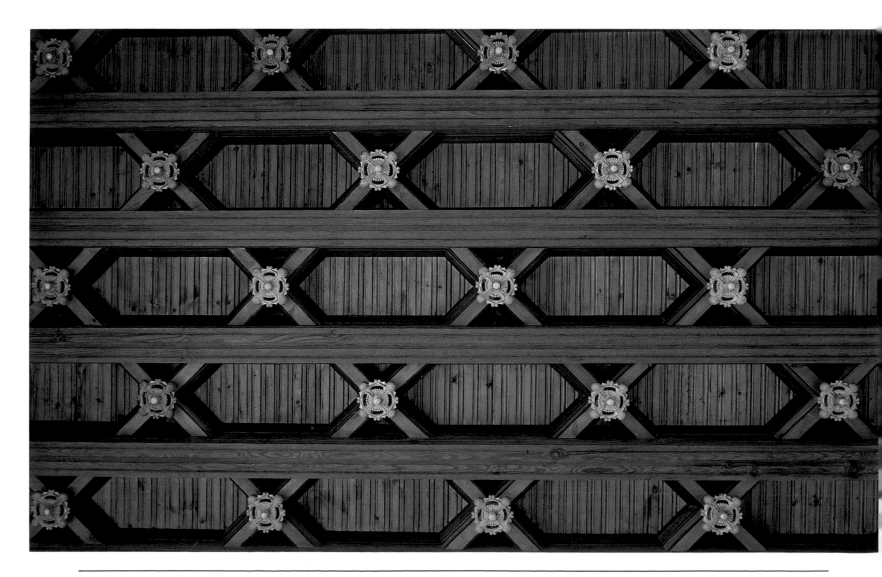

from one another only by wooden posts, which in itself makes the room seem large, an impression which is further enhanced by its height. This feature does indeed transform the house into a whim of the architect. The salon is the only room which reaches up into the attic and even takes in part of the upper split level of the ground floor, the rest of which functions as the servants' lodgings – in other words, a room which is two storeys in height, but cuts across three floors.

Gaudí's approach to the design of this house was not at all typical of him. As a rule he designed houses on the site where they were to be built, drawing additional inspiration from the location. Thus, his building projects "grew wild" in the course of their realization, sometimes taking unpredictable turns. In the case of *El Capricho* he deviated from his customary approach. He engaged his friend Cristòfol Cascante i Colom to supervise the construction of the house, never visiting the building site itself. However, he must have had detailed descriptions of the site, as his design included numerous details which were meticulously adapted to the specific conditions of the area: the house stands on a slope, and part of the site therefore had to be built up to take this into account. Gaudí designed small "pillars" to serve as the supporting walls, which resemble the minaret-like turret of the house. And the choice of colours used for the tiles is perfectly in tune with the combination of green grass and sandy ground. In future, however, Gaudí would only work in direct contact with the site and the building under construction.

Above: Balcony door in the attic of El Capricho. The crenellation-like gable is repeated on numerous windows.

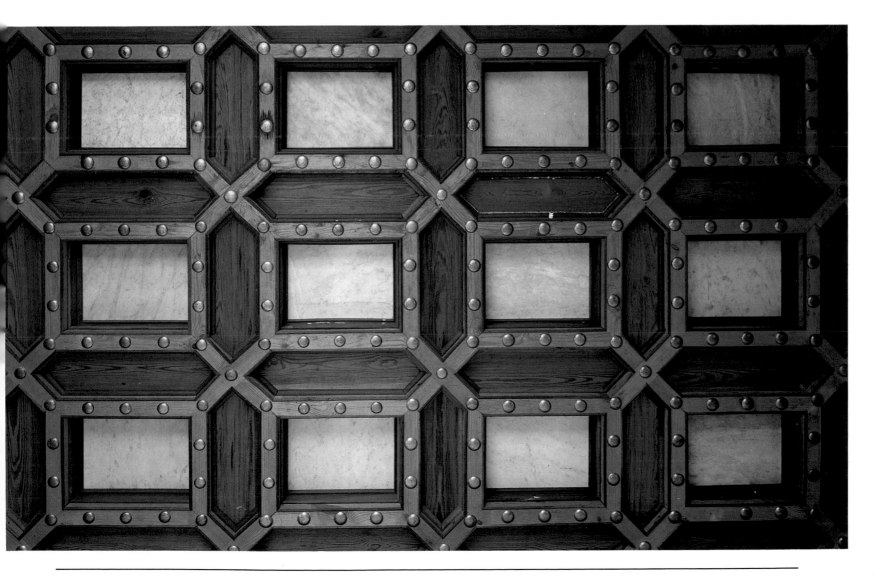

Page 54: This partial view of the front of the entrance shows Gaudí's capricious mixture of styles: left, one of the robust-looking, tower-like vaults on the outside; right, the massive-looking arching wall rises above a slender pillar in the porch with delicate ornaments between resembling Moorish designs, despite the sunflower pattern.

Left: Façade running backwards (toward the south-west). The part covered with roof tiles on the right was added in 1916.

Page 56: View of the northern façade. The balconies are decorated with wrought iron arbours and built-in benches.

Left: Carrying wall on the south side of the building. In the middle, an unroofed area for open-air conversation.

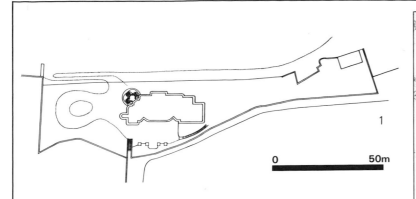

1

0   50m

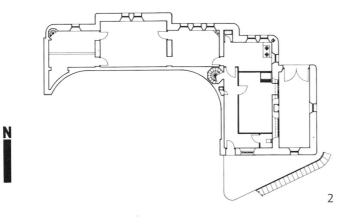

N

2

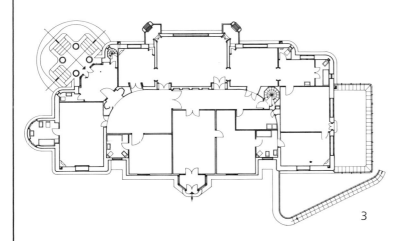

3

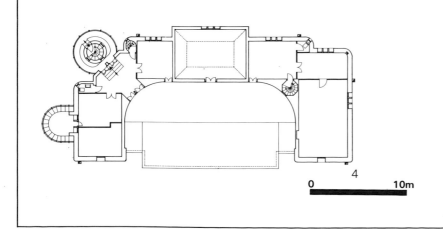

4

0   10m

A view of El Capricho from the front (top photo) suggesting the impression of a compact building with a round or square ground-plan. A view of the building from the south (bottom photo) shows the actual design of the house, also revealing the ground-plans of the individual floors. The building is essentially square, with only some variation in the structure of the upper floors owing to the arrangement of the individual rooms.

1. Layout
2. Ground-plan of the basement
3. Ground-plan of the ground floor
4. Ground-plan of the attic

The Güell Pavilions
1884-1887

Gaudí adopted a rather chilling design for his third
great architectural work. There are virtually no
outside windows, and the walls, a uniformly
designed surface decorated with light, semi-
circular ornamentation, could easily conceal a
sultan's harem. The entrance could hardly be more
austere.

On the left, the corner of a small porter's lodge
obstinately greets the visitor; on the right, the
long, flat building with the sumptuous dome
appears just as inaccessible. Anyone who is still
undaunted and nevertheless wishes to enter then
comes face to face with an iron dragon, which
bars the way, forming the mighty iron gate.
Although this imposing façade does not harbour a
royal palace, but only the stables of a country
estate, it gives some indication of the owner's
wealth all the same.

Even before Gaudí was commissioned by his friend and patron Eusebi Güell to take on the ambitious project of erecting a palace-like residence in the centre of Barcelona, he had the opportunity to offer Güell a few samples of his art. In 1883, Güell had acquired an estate outside of what was then Barcelona, between Les Corts de Sarrià and Pedralbes. Gaudí was to carry out some restoration work and construct a number of additional buildings. In keeping with Güell's wishes — one of which was to display his social standing — it was in particular the entrance that was to be given a new design. The work on the estate was carried out parallel to Gaudí's construction of the Güell Palace, but architectural worlds lie between the two projects. Although they were completed almost simultaneously, they mark two highly different phases of Gaudí's creative work. The additional buildings for the estate are clearly in line with the Mudejar style, which was also characteristic of the Casa Vicens and *El Capricho*. When Gaudí designed the ornamental exterior of the last of these three buildings, his style was in fact considerably purer than for the other two — if one can speak of stylistic purity at all in Gaudí's architecture. The light, semi-circular patterns with which he decorated the façades are one example. Gaudí used an abstract motif instead of the indigenous tagetes or sunflower patterns used in his earlier works. The little turret, which rises above the flattened dome of the riding school, is much more reserved and refined in design than the fanciful turret of *El Capricho*. Gaudí's use of a uniform pattern for the façade was his way of showing that, as far as he was concerned, the project was based on a single, coherent plan, although it consisted of such diverse buildings as stables, riding hall, and a porter's lodge.

The Pavilions bear an unmistakable resemblance to both of the Moorish works that preceded them, and yet Gaudí designed something entirely new with these three small buildings. The most fascinating aspect of them is above all the design of the interior. The porter's lodge, for example, is a single-storey octagon, but with the compactness of a cube, topped by a flattened dome – an innovation in Gaudí's formal idiom. The cupola is even repeated in the square towers adjoining the octagon. The stables are housed in a long flat building with the same ornamentation on the façade as that used in the porter's lodge: this is the only feature indicating that these two structures belong together. The adjoining riding hall, which served as a riding school, is hardly distinguishable from the stables. Only a cupola with a small tower showing Moorish inspiration alludes to its special function. The turret on the riding hall and on the porter's lodge create a kind of formal parenthesis which fuses the highly diverse buildings into a whole.

The interior design of the stables is particularly noteworthy. Connoisseurs of Gaudí's late works will be quick to notice this when visiting the estate, and may be led to think that they can detect the early signs of Gaudí's later preoccupation with high, vaulted arches. The stables are spanned by a series of thick arching walls in bright white plaster. As a result, they look amazingly expansive, wide and light. However, these arches do not take an extreme, parabolic form. They do not so much anticipate Gaudí's later carrying arches as hark back to the factory hall in Mataró. Nevertheless, the design is bold and modern in effect. Above all, it is surprisingly down-to-earth compared with the rich decor of the outside walls.

However, the gate that runs between the porter's lodge and the stables is probably more impressive than the stables themselves. It is an eminent example of Gaudí's talent for ironwork. It is also one of the first major examples of the Art Nouveau elements in his work. Moreover, it is proof of Gaudí's great skills as a designer and structural engineer. It is 15 feet wide and yet consists of only a single piece; in other words, it is hinged on only one side. Gaudí thus had to use a very tall hinge pole – more than 30 feet high. If Gaudí had designed the gate symmetrically – as was commonly the case – it would have looked like the gate to a prison. But instead he set the top of the iron gate at a little more than half of the 30-foot height, lending it a fanciful elegance. The lower half of the gate consists of a pattern made of little square metal plates which looks very transluscent. Above it, in a multitude of sweeping lines, rises a huge dragon with terrifying gaping jaws; this gave the gate its name and is also an early example of the

The so-called Dragon Gate at the entrance to the Güell Pavilions was probably inspired by the myth of the Hesperides. According to this myth, a winged dragon guarded the garden in which three beautiful nymphs lived. Hercules succeeded in conquering the dragon and gained entrance to the garden.

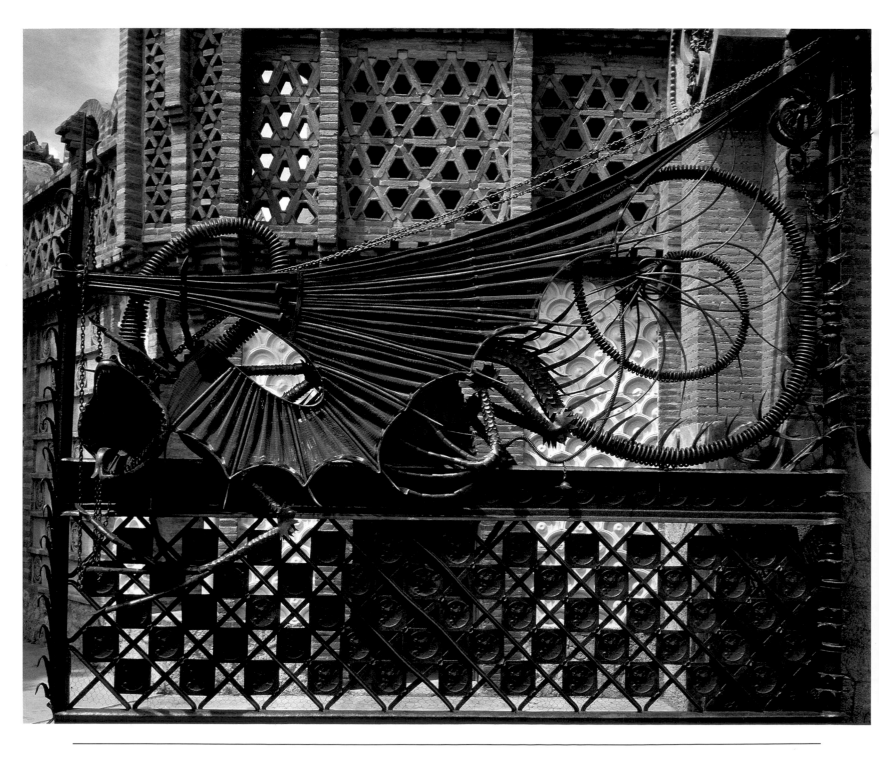

Left: The outside walls of the porter's lodge and the stables are decorated with honeycomb patterns.

Above: Detailed photo of the Dragon Gate. Like a forbidding guard from the underworld, the dragon bares its jaws to any would-be intruder.

Left: Decorative pattern on the outside wall of the riding hall.

Page 64: Upper section of the hinge pole on the Dragon Gate. The top of the pole is sculpted with imaginative ornamentation patterned after the dense branches and leaves of an orange tree. While perhaps not noticeable at first glance, the mortar joints between the bricks of the hinge pole are filled ·with multi-coloured ceramic fragments.

Page 65: Entrance to the stables which house the Gaudí Chair at the College of Architecture (right).

Right: View from the porter's lodge onto the stable area and the cupola of the riding hall. The roof of the stables is covered with a row of white pipes. Variations on this element reappear in the Sagrada Família parish school.

Page 68: Interior of the riding hall – a prime example of Gaudí's feel for lighting. The light, bare inside wall evenly reflects the glistening light which falls through the windows in the cupola.

symbolism in Gaudí's work: the dragon watches over the garden, and fanciful though it may seem, owing to the myriads of Art Nouveau twirls, it nevertheless fulfils its function very effectively: whenever anyone tries to open the gate, the dragon's claw rises up with its strong iron talons.

These are the major works that Gaudí designed for the Güell estate. Several of the plans for the numerous minor projects – which included redesigning the old Güell residence and a perimeter wall for the cemetery – were eventually withdrawn. They are only of secondary importance and come nowhere close to matching the quality of the dragon gate, which ranks as a masterpiece of Catalonian ironwork to the present day.

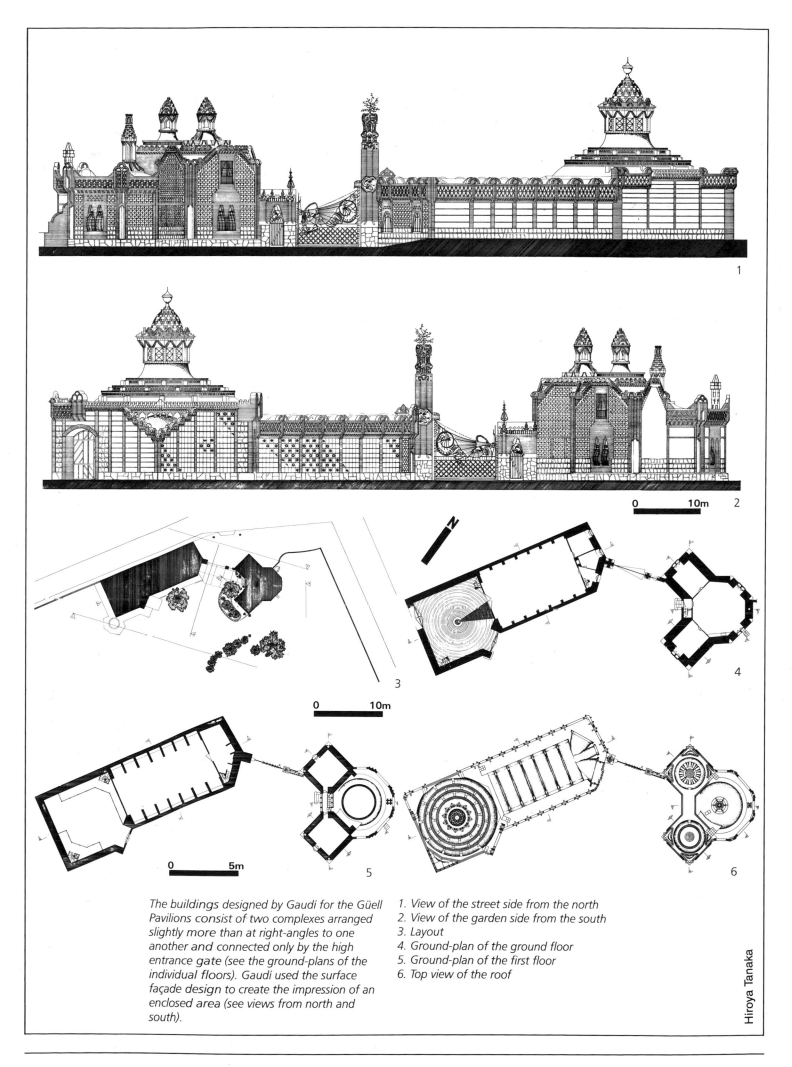

The buildings designed by Gaudí for the Güell Pavilions consist of two complexes arranged slightly more than at right-angles to one another and connected only by the high entrance gate (see the ground-plans of the individual floors). Gaudí used the surface façade design to create the impression of an enclosed area (see views from north and south).

1. View of the street side from the north
2. View of the garden side from the south
3. Layout
4. Ground-plan of the ground floor
5. Ground-plan of the first floor
6. Top view of the roof

Hiroya Tanaka

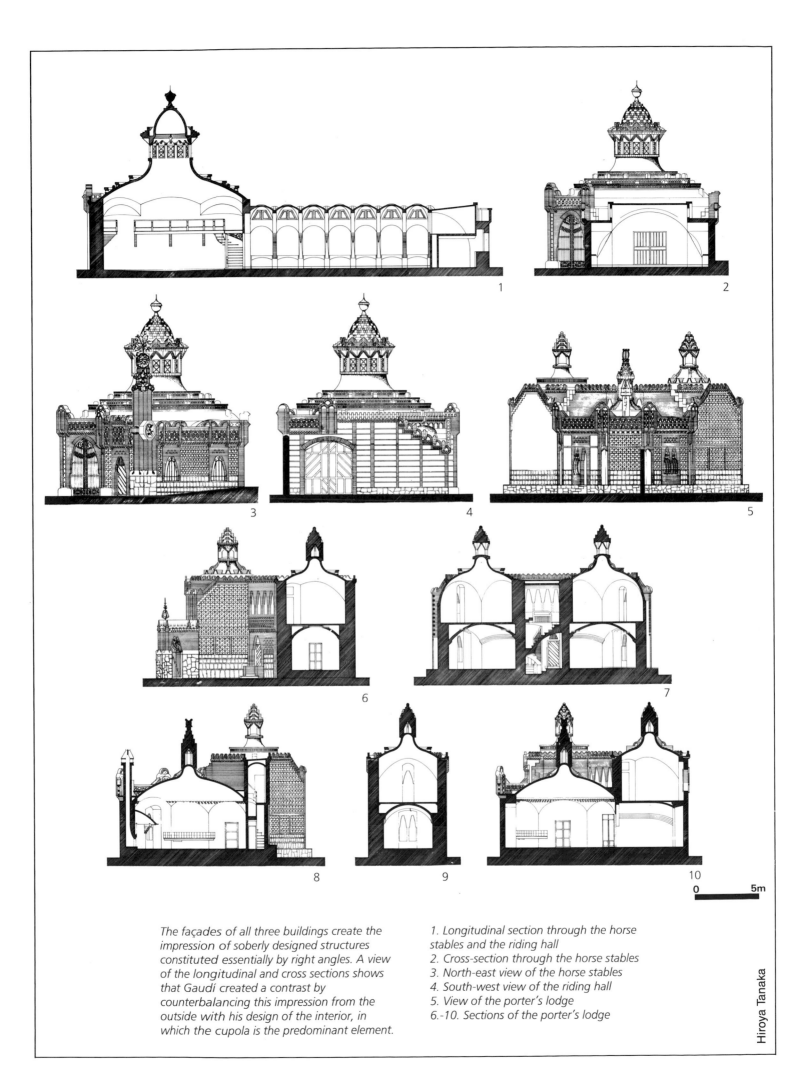

1

2

3   4   5

6   7

8   9   10

0 ——— 5m

The façades of all three buildings create the impression of soberly designed structures constituted essentially by right angles. A view of the longitudinal and cross sections shows that Gaudí created a contrast by counterbalancing this impression from the outside with his design of the interior, in which the cupola is the predominant element.

1. Longitudinal section through the horse stables and the riding hall
2. Cross-section through the horse stables
3. North-east view of the horse stables
4. South-west view of the riding hall
5. View of the porter's lodge
6.-10. Sections of the porter's lodge

Hiroya Tanaka

Güell Palace

1886–1889

No matter where one stands in the Calle Nou de la Rambla, it is difficult to get a full view of the palace Gaudí built for his friend Eusebi Güell. Not because of its size: the site is only 54 x 66 feet. The most one would normally build on a piece of land this size is a respectable middle-class home. However, the street is so narrow that it is impossible to step back far enough to have a good view of the entire palace (which, incidentally, is not in the best of neighbourhoods). All one can see from one of the houses across the road is a plain front made of large stone blocks. One sees little of the lavishly decorated facade on the lower floors, but cannot help noticing on the palace roof the bizarre turrets which adorned all the chimneys subsequently designed by Gaudí. This is a palace with a fairy-tale garden on the roof.

When Gaudí became Eusebi Güell's favourite architect in the mid-1880s, he had very few works to his name. The Casa Vicens was still in progress, and *El Capricho* was about to be completed. The businessman's appreciation for Gaudí's work was actually based on the samples he had seen at the Paris World Fair. Many were the times in Gaudí's life that his patrons demonstrated their confidence in his work, even though his style had yet to mature and prove itself. Güell sensed the extent of Gaudí's talent, but he was surely also attracted to Gaudí because of the young architect's social commitment to the working classes and his Catalonian convictions. Gaudí, for his part, was fascinated by Güell's rare combination of nobility, financial power, and commitment to the cause of the lower classes. When he designed a coat of arms for Güell, he added the words: "Yesterday a shepherd, today a man of nobility," to put Güell's career in a nutshell — a man who had grown up in humble circumstances, but later returned from a stay in America with a sizable fortune to his name. When he commissioned Gaudí to build a palace in the middle of Barcelona, money was no longer an object. At one point, an employee in charge of managing Güell's finances once called the art patron's attention to the enormous rise in the project's costs. "I fill Don Eusebio's pockets," he is said to have lamented, "and Gaudí then empties them." This criticism, however, fell on deaf ears.

In return, of course, Güell acquired something of value which could not be measured in money. Yet the conditions were anything but favourable. The Conde del Asalto (known today as Calle Nou de la Rambla) where the palace was to be erected is a narrow street, and the construction site was by no means large: 54 x 66 feet is not much space for an average palace, not even for an urban palace. Gaudí drafted no less than 25 plans for the façade alone. He finally decided on a design which was a surprisingly reserved, austere version of his previous works. The front of the house,

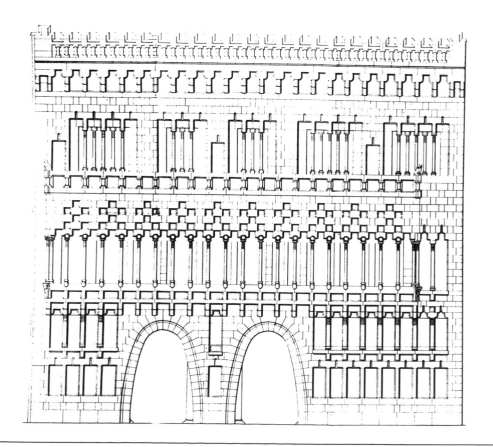

Calle del Conde del Asalto nº 3 y 5

Escala de 1 per 70

Barcelona 5 de Junio 1886
El Arquitecto
Gaudí

El propietario
Eusebi Güell

0   5m

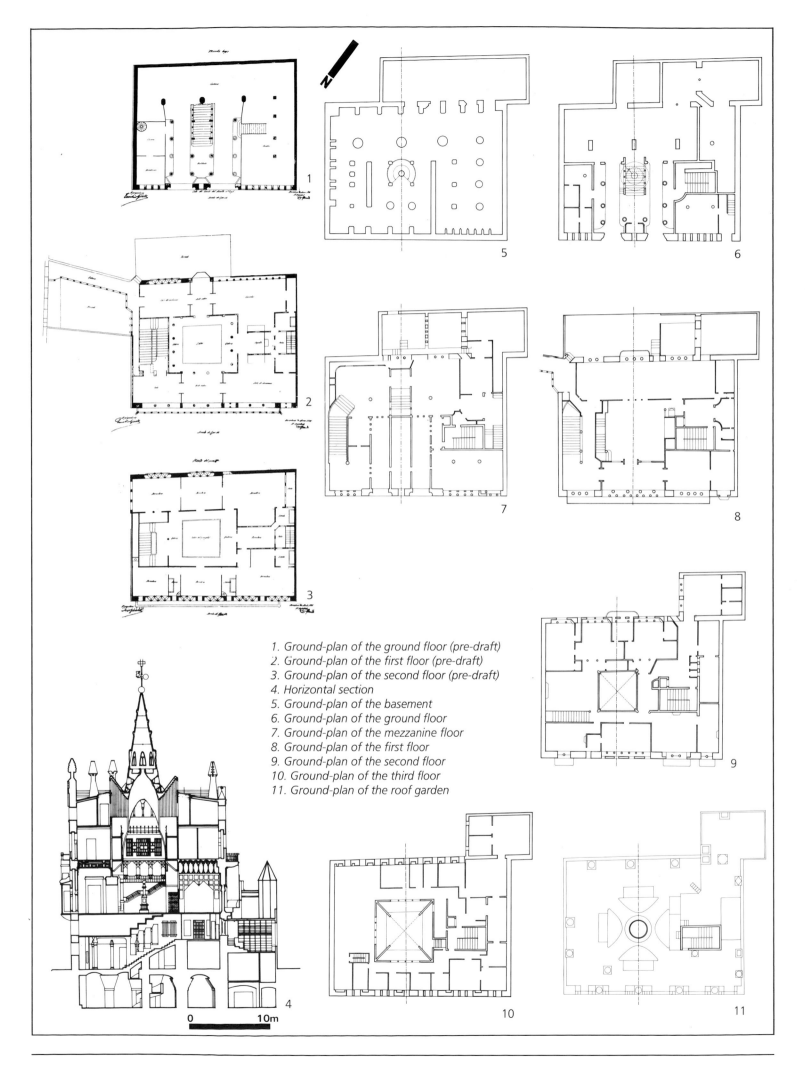

1. Ground-plan of the ground floor (pre-draft)
2. Ground-plan of the first floor (pre-draft)
3. Ground-plan of the second floor (pre-draft)
4. Horizontal section
5. Ground-plan of the basement
6. Ground-plan of the ground floor
7. Ground-plan of the mezzanine floor
8. Ground-plan of the first floor
9. Ground-plan of the second floor
10. Ground-plan of the third floor
11. Ground-plan of the roof garden

0   10m

Page 74-75: The main front entrance consists of two adjacent gate arches with cast iron gates. Between the gates there are allusions to the Catalonian coat of arms.

Page 77: Mirror table designed by Gaudí for the Güell Palace.

Pages 78-79: Main air vent in the grand hall on the main floor (first floor). In the middle, the stairwell leading to the second floor.

Below: Spire of the conical turret rising from the cupola on the central room of the house (left). The chimneys and ventilation ducts are scattered over the surface of the roof, creating an original pattern; one is reminded of a little forest of cypress trees (right).

which directly joins the adjacent building, is characterized by right angles, and the main decoration is the slightly protruding balcony on the first floor, which extends to the second floor only at the ends. Gaudí almost completely dispensed with sculptural ornamentation; only between the two large entrance ways did he add a lavishly designed column bearing the emblem of Catalonia – a clear allusion to his patron's political leanings (as well as his own). Because of this austere façade with its clear lines, covered with grey polished marble plates, the palace looks larger than it actually is. It resembles somewhat the urban palaces in Renaissance Venice; perhaps this was Gaudí's way of erecting a monument to Güell's mother, who came from Italy – albeit, not from the nobility.

This historicizing façade is, however, broken up by an extremely anachronistic element. Two enormous gates made of iron lattice rise before the visitor's eyes, who in the narrow street cannot step back far enough to appreciate its full effect. (This is why these gates are frequently photographed from one side, usually with a wide-angle lens, which makes it seem as if they were leaning backward.) These gates became quite an attraction because they were the first of their kind in Barcelona and therefore bound to meet with scepticism and rejection. Eventually, such gates became quite commonplace. They are only one example of the way Gaudí set architectural trends. The gates have a peculiar arch shape which is neither pointed and Gothic nor rounded and Arabic, a type of arch which had such a strong influence on Gaudí's first works. This was the first time

Page 80: Grand hall on the main floor. The wings of the entrance gates to the house chapel and the surface of the walls are decorated with paintings by Alejo Clapès. In the upper part of the picture one can see the balcony on the second floor.

Page 81: Upper part of the cupola in the grand hall. The surface is covered with hectagonal, flat stones. A multitude of round holes let light through, making the cupola look like a starry sky.

Page 83: Three large parabolic arches formed by grey stone pillars stand in front of the living and dining-room windows. The polished snake-eye stone pillars shine in the light.

Below: Sofa designed by Gaudí. Inspired by Art Nouveau, Gaudí designed various pieces of furniture for the palace. The sofa pictured here is part of the bedroom furnishings on the second floor.

that Gaudí employed the parabolic arch design which would reappear in all of his subsequent works and which he would later develop into a carrying element of his buildings. (This element made it possible for him to do without the flying buttresses and arches he disliked so much in Gothic architecture.) The parabolic forms appear once more in the interior of the building, where Gaudí even experimented with the Gothic tradition. In the lobby on the main floor of the palace, the light that falls through the windows is subdued by three huge parabolic arches formed by grey, smoothly polished stone pillars. The towering arches create the impression of a Gothic window; but the windows which Gaudí employed in Güell's palace are rectangular – in other words, serve as a counterpoint to the lines of the arches. In this lobby Gaudí again broke with predominant forms of architecture – a break which was initiated by the round archway he had used on the outside façade.

These arches also reveal the first signs of his preoccupation with Art Nouveau. The upper third is decorated with rich ornamentation made of winding iron bars in which one can see the owner's initials; they are framed by a twisting line which strongly resembles a horse-whip. This was Gaudí's reference to the actual function of these gates, which at the same time justified their completely disproportionate size: they were designed to enable guests to ride through this entrance way in their carriages. In the lobby, he designed a gently sloping ramp for the horses, leading down to the sub-level, i.e. the stables. Like the gate design, this was also an innovation in Barcelona's architecture. Gaudí's real debut as an architect in this city – the Casa Vicens was located more on the outskirts, in the Gràcia district – was breathtaking. The Art Nouveau elements of the entrance gate were also repeated inside the building. For one thing, there are lavish decorations on the pillars, of which there are a considerable number: from the thick, supporting, mushroom-shaped pillars in the basement all the way to the elegant, expensive, smoothly polished grey pillars made of snake-eye stone excavated from a quarry in the Pyrenees. There are a total of 127 pillars in the palace, which generally created the impression of overwhelming size – an optical illusion for which Gaudí was in all likelihood deliberately striving. Indeed, he was quite willing to allow for distorted proportions in order to achieve this. The entrance portals are out of all proportion to the surface area of the façade as a whole. Yet, when one stands before them, one cannot help but have the feeling that one is viewing a palace of immeasurable size. One has a similar impression when climbing the steps to the first main floor (the building has six floors in all). A hall spanning three floors forms the centre of the building. It replaces, as it were, the normal inner courtyard, but at the same time creates the impression that one is standing in a huge Baroque church. This room is covered by a cupola in which Gaudí put numerous round holes. Thus, it looks as if starlight was falling directly into the building. As grandiose as this middle room may seem, however, it only has a surface of 27 square feet, and a height of 52 feet. It is this height that makes the hall look so overwhelming. And it is here that social life takes place. Gaudí designed an organ for the music-lover Güell, placing the pipes in the upper gallery. The music thus seems to cascade down over the listeners from on high. An altar rounds out the design of this unique room, which was originally intended to play only a marginal role. However, in the course of the planning the architect and

owner alike became so enthusiastic with regard to the room that it eventually became the heart and soul of the building. It seems as if the other rooms of the house, of which there are no small number, were built around it: it is a kind of hyper-dimensional pillar which "bears" the rest of the building.

The other rooms are, of course, not merely of secondary importance. Gaudí took great care in designing the ceilings, which are lavishly decorated with wooden ornamentation, eucalyptus and cypress panels, complemented (and at the same time supported) by richly decorated iron components; there are no stable elements bearing the weight of the ceiling. In addition to the architectural design of the building itself, the furniture designed by Gaudí is particularly noteworthy because it reflects his very own version of Art Nouveau. There are the typical fanciful forms, yet they are accompanied by surprisingly plain forms. The mirror on the dressing table on the upper floor looks like a collage of traditional rectangular mirrors with elegant twirls of Art Nourveau at its base, thus combining two totally different styles of mirrors. The two wooden elements on which it rests – or seems to be balanced, actually – are no less original. They are little pillars; and the feet look like oddly bent, surreal three-dimensional figures. In the case of later buildings, the workers were often very sceptical about Gaudí's designs and asked how they were supposed to stay standing. The same question inevitably comes to mind when one views the dressing table. It seems as if the mirror is about to fall down at any moment.

The twisted legs of the table recur in the building itself, namely, on the roof. The roof was always an important element for Gaudí, and he gave his fertile imagination free rein in designing it. And it never bothered him that the forms, many of which are quite bizarre, could usually not be seen from the street. The roof is topped by a small cupola which rises above the hall in the centre and tapers off into a pointed tower, lending the building a peculiarly religious air. Yet the tower clashes completely with the rest of the building – even in its colour; it is simply stuck on the top. It is surrounded by 18 surrealistic "sculptures" which remind one of the legs of the dressing table. They are early examples of the little turrets Gaudí was later to sublimate in the form of the mitre-like spires of the Sagrada Familia: small, often twisted formations with additional ornamental points and corners, which look like sheer playfulness and yet, as so often in Gaudí's works, serve highly practical purposes – they are both chimney decorations and ventilation ducts. Gaudí detracted from the ordinary function of these elements by adding the lavish ornamentation of colourful tiles.

This palace immediately wrested Gaudí from anonymity. During the construction work (from 1886 to 1889, an amazingly short time) numerous reports appeared in the press (even in American newspapers) which at first only named the owner of the house, but soon turned their attention to the young architect as well, who had set out so unabashedly on an entirely new architectural path.

Page 84: The ceiling in the living and dining room is made of beechwood.

Above: Gaudí used several parabolic arches to subdue the glaring light from outside.

Below: Basement with thick supporting pillars and the spiral-shaped ramp for carriages.

Colegio Teresiano

1888–1889

Basking in the rays of sun from the south and
against the background of a blue sky, the building
radiantly shines forth in all its splendour. The large
coat of arms of the order housed here — the Order
of St. Theresa of Avila — stands out colourfully. But
the impression is deceptive. Frugality and austerity
were the highest commandments of the order,
and Gaudí, too, had to abide by them. Thus, the
balcony, which rises like a tower above the
entrance, is nearly the only decoration in what is,
by Gaudí's standards, an ascetic structure. Only
the parapet, which runs in a zig-zag pattern along
the edge of the roof, is pure pomp. But it is also
representative of the style of the building as a
whole, which was devoted completely to the saint
who gave the order its name, and St. Theresa was
guided by mediaeval philosophy, the pinnacle
of the Gothic style. Gaudí followed suit in his own
manner.

Page 87: Outside view from the schoolyard.

Page 89: Part of the balcony in the middle of the main façade. The coat of arms of the Carmelite order is affixed in the middle of the first floor with the cross on Mt. Carmel; the hearts of the Virgin Mary and of St. Theresa at its sides.

Page 90/91: These corridors on the first floor encompass the interior courtyard. Natural light is skilfully captured by the walls which are washed in white limestone, creating a shiny effect.

Below: Windows on the ground floor of the main façade (left). Turret and coat of arms of the Carmelite order.

While still a student and young architect, Gaudí would never have dreamed that he would one day construct religious buildings requiring him to bend his principles of form entirely to suit the wishes of religious clients. True to the trends of the time, he tended to be anti-clerical in sentiment. In all likelihood, the contract to design the Sagrada Familia at first intrigued him purely for architectural reasons — quite apart from the fact that as an aspiring young architect he could hardly afford to turn down such a challenging project. The designs for his secular buildings showed him to be rather more an architect of unbridled temperament. The fact that at the end of the 1880s he took on the task of designing a school and mother-house for the Order of St. Theresa (of Avila) in Barcelona indicates that his attitude toward the Church had changed. For the conditions were far from favourable. As for the costs, Gaudí had been accustomed to having abundant resources at his disposal for the design of his first works; even in the the Casa Vicens project, where the owner had not had limitless means available, money had not been an object. When he tackled the project for the convent, he was still spending money left and right for the Güell palace. The Colegio Teresiano was another matter altogether, as the order had made frugality its prime commandment. The budget allocated for Gaudí's work was not lavish. The fact that he kept to this budget shows the extent to which he always adjusted his building plans to the modalities at hand — be it to the local conditions of the building site or the message the structure was to convey (such as the historical past of Catalonia, which he incorpo-

Page 93: Corridor on the first floor. The effective use of whitewashed surfaces is a typical element of the Mudéjar style.

rated into the design of Bellesguard). Gaudí was nevertheless not spared several critical remarks made by Father Rev. Enric d'Ossó i Cervelló, the founder of the order. When the latter admonished him because of the expense, Gaudí revealed his obstinate temperament: "To each his own, Father Enric," he is supposed to have replied. "I build houses, you read masses and say prayers."

The order was still very young, having only been founded in 1876. The target of criticism was the mounting bills for bricks, and not without justification. Gaudí's work on the Colegio Teresiano was not only subject to tight constraints in terms of the available budget; the Order's ideal of poverty by definition incorporated the ideals of austerity, sobriety, and frugality in every respect. Gaudí on the whole abided by this rule, even though it must have been difficult for him to do so. Nor was he at liberty to pursue any design he wished. The first floor of the Order's building was already standing; in other words, as in the case of the Sagrada Familia, Gaudí had to proceed from a design that was not his own, only in this case it was much more confining. The entire shape of the ground-plan of the house had been prescribed: a strictly rectangular, drawn-out building. The floors constructed above it, however, bear Gaudí's unmistakable mark. The ground-plan divides the building lengthwise into three narrow sections which run parallel to each other. The basement of the middle section includes a long, narrow corridor; just above this, on the ground floor,

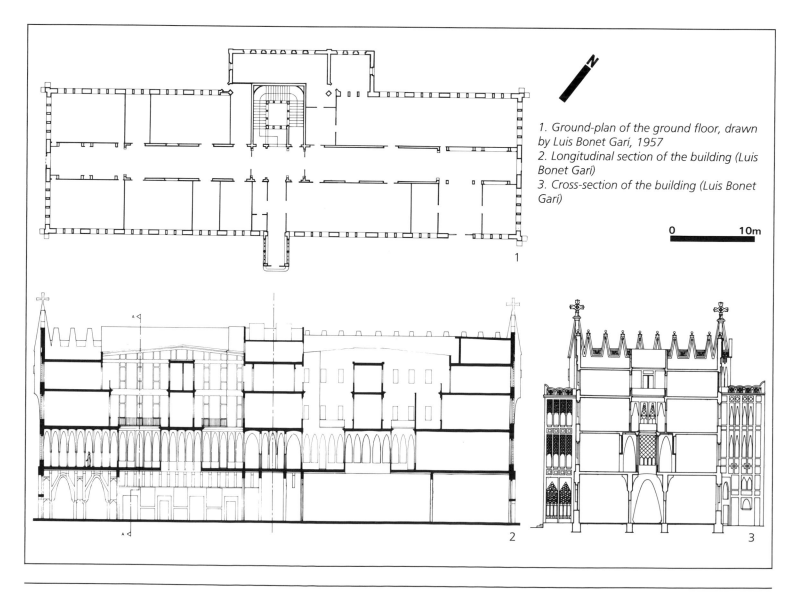

1. Ground-plan of the ground floor, drawn by Luis Bonet Garí, 1957
2. Longitudinal section of the building (Luis Bonet Garí)
3. Cross-section of the building (Luis Bonet Garí)

0   10m

One of the many letter symbols Gaudí used to refer to Jesus – usually in the wrought-iron window grating.

Parabolic arches made of brick. Using the simplest of materials and a slight variation of the same basic forms Gaudí created an impression of Spartanic sobriety as well as great architectonic complexity.

rectangular inner courtyards allow the light to shine in the rooms on the inside. These inner courtyards are continued on the upper floors. Normally, such a construction on the inside of a building would have required two carrying walls along the length of it – which in fact exist, on the ground floor. However, Gaudí altered the supporting structure on the remaining floors. Instead of the carrying walls he employed long corridors consisting of a single row of symmetrical, identical parabolic arches. In so doing, Gaudí accomplished several things at once: first of all, he eliminated the need for a carrying structure based on a long, uninteresting-looking wall; this way, he introduced some variety into the rigid lines of the building, which was already austere enough as it was. Secondly, he created generous corridors which almost form a kind of cloister, owing to the series of parallel arches. These arches are whitewashed, with numerous windows spaced between them, opening onto the inner courtyard. As a result, the corridor is brightly, but indirectly, lit; the light is evenly distributed, lending the hall a quiet, contemplative atmosphere. At the same time, the all-pervading arch design alludes to the Gothic style, and thus, to a period which was also a focal point for the Carmelite order founded by St. Theresa. In fact, Gaudí made this arch design the pivotal stylistic element of the building. Pointed arches dominate the overall appearance. The outer façade along the entire upper floor is marked by a row of pointed arch designs of various heights. The protruding covered balcony at the entrance, which breaks up the strict rectangular line of the ground-plan, contains pointed arch windows, and the windows of the other floors resemble pointed arches as well. However, Gaudí also introduced a counterbalance to this underlying Gothic element: the window shutters, which are usually closed, repeat the rectangular form of the ground-plan. The balcony over the entrance is also primarily characterized by rectangular designs.

Gaudí accomplished all this with simple and above all inexpensive materials. Large blocks of undressed stone alternate with broad sections of brick wall. Nevertheless, Ossó's criticism was justified. Gaudí permitted himself a certain amount of luxury in a few places, even if only with this quite inexpensive material. For example, along the top floor he added a row of brick parapets, again drawing on the underlying Gothic style, as a decorative finish to the façade. Thus, a delicate row of zigzags rises up against the horizon. His use of false brick arches in the large hall spaces was another luxury. They have no carrying function, but lend the halls a ceremonial and somewhat old-fashioned touch. Without these added touches the building might have been more in keeping with the basic principles of the order, but the halls would have been too bare. Gaudí combined whitewashed sections of wall with brick walls and in this way created a synthesis of the ascetic and of rustic, simple homeliness. From the strict standpoint of the order, the only thing for which he could be taken to task would be the spiralled, inward-turning brick pillars which are a bit reminiscent of the spiralling chimneys on the roof of the Güell Palace (which later also reappear as the bosses on the bell towers of the Sagrada Familia). This was the only playful excursion into the realm of the purely ornamental which Gaudí allowed himself.

On the other hand, he kept entirely to the main principle of the order. Gaudí's work on the convent marks the beginning of his steadily growing preoccupation with symbolic references. For example, he topped the pointed parapets on the roof with small mortarboards, a sign of his reverence for St. Theresa, the scholar. However, they were soon removed (in 1936). The order's coat of arms appears six times, the most lavish instance being on the balcony in the middle of the main façade. St. Theresa's initials also appear six times in the wrought-iron grating. A band of two brick layers runs between the upper floors in the middle of the undressed stone front to the outer façade, and the initials of the name Jesus are burnt into the ceramic plates. These initials appear a total of 127 times in ceramic, and another 35 times on wrought-iron gratings. One can count many more. Such references could be interpreted as pure playfulness, but Gaudí integrated such allusions discreetly. One has to look very closely in order to find them. In this way, the building becomes a little mystery; the "revelation" is concealed. It is necessary to become deeply engrossed in exploring the secrets of the building, which in a sense make it an embodiment of the order's saint: the house of the mystic is itself a small mystery. It is questionable whether all of its contemporaries recognized it for what it was. Otherwise, people would not have been so quick to remove one of its most genuinely symbolic elements, namely, the mortarboards (which were probably taken merely as a quirk of the architect, a man already known for his bizarre sense of architectonic humour).

Spiralling pillars in the dining-hall on the ground floor (left). Passageway and main corridor on the ground floor (right).

Casa Calvet

1898–1900

Gaudí indeed made a name for himself as a master
of magnificent, lavish works; yet most of his
architectural creations were surprisingly small and
often served quite trivial purposes. The Casa Calvet
was to serve as both commercial premises and a
residence. Perhaps this is why Gaudí displayed
such reserve in designing it – the Casa Calvet (in
the Calle de Casp in Barcelona) is his most
conventional work. And it was precisely for this
building that he received a prize from the city; it
was the only official recognition he ever received.
Perhaps the building authorities were relieved that,
in designing this house situated in the middle of
Barcelona's elegant residential district, Gaudí had
refrained from the architectural extravagances that
characterized his previous works. Nevertheless, a
bit of eccentricity found its way into this work: the
heads of three saints on the upper floor look
defiantly down, they are richly-decorated hoists –
and the height of the house exceeded the officially
prescribed limit.

Above: An artistically designed oriel on the main façade above the main entrance.

Page 97: Façade of the Casa Calvet, seen from the Calle de Casp.

Page 99: Rear view of the Casa Calvet. Open and covered balconies alternate. As on the façade, the intended effect of rhythmic repetition comes to the fore.

Page 100: Entrance hall with lift and stairs.

Gaudí began work in 1898 on the structure at 52, Calle de Casp (today, the house number is 48), a residence of considerable dimensions. It was not his first attempt at this genre. In the early 1890s he had constructed a large combined commercial and private villa for Don Mariano Andrés and Don Simón Fernández in León which, in terms of its purpose, was quite similar to the new project in Barcelona: commercial premises in the lower part, with apartments from the first floor upwards. The house in León contained two larger and four smaller flats. The building is imposing in size and looks impressive, not really like a private home, but rather more like a palace. The neighbourhood had something to do with this: immediately adjacent to it – the Casa de los Botines – was the palace of the Guzmanes. Gaudí took this into consideration somewhat by adding to the sides of the building rounded oriels which rise upward like towers and, owing to the tapered, round roofs, add an intriguing touch to the otherwise more matter-of-fact overall roof design. In León, moreover, Gaudí had the option of constructing a house that stood on its own – something which could not be taken for granted in the city – and bordered on the Plaza de San Marcelo on two sides.

In the Calle de Casp in Barcelona the conditions were much less favourable. Gaudí had to fit the building into a row of existing structures without leaving any gaps. This was a new experience for him, as even on the Casa Vicens project, a building closed in on all sides, he had been able to create a significant amount of room space by a shrewd division of the area he had to work with. This made the house look larger and more spacious than it actually is. By comparison, the Casa Calvet (named after the patrons, the heirs of Pere Màrtir Calvet) is almost delicate in appearance. It is squeezed in tightly between the houses on either side. And, owing to the conditions of the site, Gaudí in fact immediately ran into difficulties with the neighbours. The nuns living in the convent close-by had a provisional court injunction put on the building work, whereupon Gaudí put up a "screen" in the inner courtyard shielding the work from vision, thus again showing how practically-minded he was. The "screen" blocks almost everything from view and yet allows an amazing amount of light to come in through numerous, carefully designed holes: the holes are shaped at the top like flattened arches, creating the effect of shutters.

Despite the relatively limited amount of space available, the house was meant to accomodate many different purposes. The cellar and ground floor were to serve, much the same as in León, as storage space and business premises. The upper floors were to contain eight apartments. Accordingly, Gaudí built – unlike in León – more upwards than outwards. Four floors rise above the ground floor. In order to find room for all the designated purposes, Gaudí designed what by his standards was a very simple building, with a nearly symmetrical ground-plan. Two, almost square, equally large inner courtyards meet at the stairwell; two further oblong, rectangular courtyards are situated on the sides. Their function is above all to provide light for the flats.

The Casa Calvet is certainly the most conventional of all Gaudí's works and, in terms of its overall structure, almost boring. The fact that he came into conflict with the municipal building authorities because of it is something of a tragic irony. The top of the building has two elegantly crafted gable tops which, however, overshot the maximum height for which

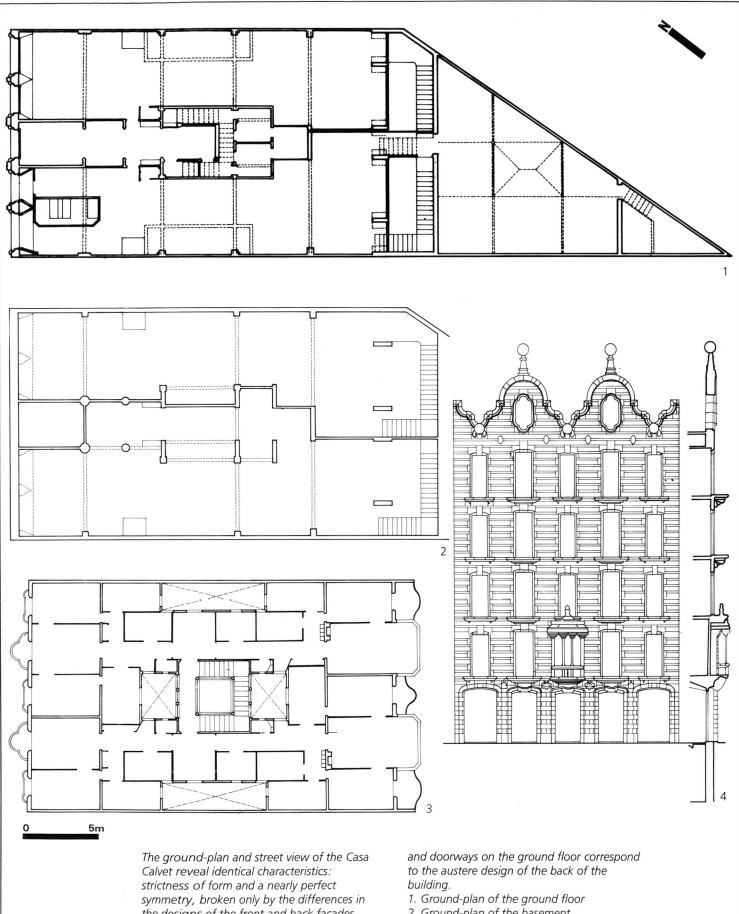

The ground-plan and street view of the Casa Calvet reveal identical characteristics: strictness of form and a nearly perfect symmetry, broken only by the differences in the designs of the front and back façades. Details of the façade structure also appear in the ground-plan: the gable-like projection of the roof corresponds formally with the barrelled balconies on the front façade, whereas the large, soberly-designed windows and doorways on the ground floor correspond to the austere design of the back of the building.

1. Ground-plan of the ground floor
2. Ground-plan of the basement
3. Ground-plan of the second, third and fourth floors
4. Frontal view of the façade and section through the façade (drawing submitted for approval)

permission had been granted. Even in the case of this relatively austere building, this feature was surely an expression of Gaudí's perpetual strokes of wit, or of perpetual obstinacy, for he could have easily dispensed with the gables; they are ornamental additions like the little towers on the Casa Vicens or the superfluous arabesque tower of *El Capricho*. Gaudí was also obstinate in his manner of dealing with this conflict. Whereas he had found an expedient means of dealing with the protests of the neighbouring nuns, he would not budge an inch for the authorities. He threatened to simply cut off the façade exactly at the legally prescribed height; any modification of the design was out of the question. He got his way in the end, and in fact

Above: Ceiling of the salon with flower patterns. There are decorative wooden ceilings of this type throughout the house.

Page 103: Gaudí created an artistic wall design. Floral Art Nouveau-like drawings are placed in sharp contrast to austere, stone-edged windows and doors; bright blue tiles contrast with the sober sections of brick wall.

even "topped" it all off with two crosses, lending the otherwise plain rectangular building a certain lightness, an upward thrust. In fact, he applied all of his creative energy to the design of these upper sections. The heads of three martyrs gaze down from the gables onto the street. He also used the gables to attach an extremely useful hoist which can be employed to lift furniture.

It was in keeping with Gaudí's obstinate manner that he situated all of these elements so high up the building that they are hardly visible from the street. When the Güells stopped by one day to look at the building during the construction work, Güell's wife asked unabashedly what the peculiar "snarls" up on the roof were supposed to be; Gaudí answered in his usual

Despatx

brooding manner that those were crosses, indeed "snarls and, for many people, a source of irritation."

Less conspicuous, but no less impressive in effect is the overall design of the façades. The Casa Calvet looks much larger than the austere, straight buildings surrounding it – not only because of the two gables on top. This may have something to do with the many balconies and their rounded, barrelling ironwork, which make it seem as if the whole façade of the house were bulging forth. Gaudí must have deliberately set out to achieve this effect, for although the Casa Calvet as a whole is almost symmetrical, the balconies are of various designs. Those along the sides are smaller and also not as bulging as those in the middle. Moreover, he placed a huge oriel above the main entrance in the middle of the building that was almost baroque in design. This is the most manifest example of his predisposition to symbolic allusion, which was to take its clearest form in the Sagrada Familia. The family coat of arms adorns the entrance, as does a cypress tree, the symbol of hospitality.

But the house also derives volume from the use of a material – large blocks of undressed stone – which Gaudí had previously employed only in combination with other materials. The irregular surface of the large stone blocks prevents the façade from appearing flat, an impression which, because of the plain design, could have arisen quite easily. Here, too, much can be gleaned from drawing a comparison: in this building, with its pronounced symmetrical structure, it would not have been unusual for the design of the rear façade to match that of the front. And in principle, this is also the case. However, instead of the roundish, barrelling balconies, there are two rows of galleries enclosed in glass (with double-paned shuttered

Page 104: Bench and large mirror in the entrance hall. The blue tile covering is striking.

Page 106/107: Gaudí designed more of the furnishings for the Casa Calvet than for the Güell Palace. In particular, the chairs (page 107) were designed with the human body in mind.

Below: Cut and polished oak furniture, designed by Gaudí.

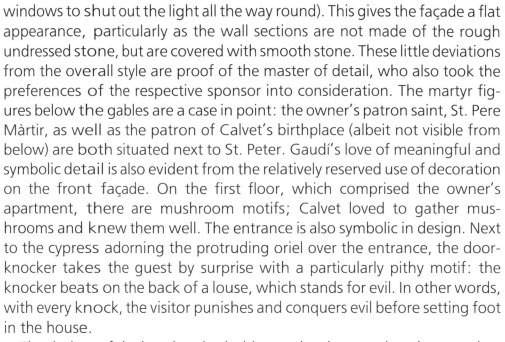

windows to shut out the light all the way round). This gives the façade a flat appearance, particularly as the wall sections are not made of the rough undressed stone, but are covered with smooth stone. These little deviations from the overall style are proof of the master of detail, who also took the preferences of the respective sponsor into consideration. The martyr figures below the gables are a case in point: the owner's patron saint, St. Pere Màrtir, as well as the patron of Calvet's birthplace (albeit not visible from below) are both situated next to St. Peter. Gaudí's love of meaningful and symbolic detail is also evident from the relatively reserved use of decoration on the front façade. On the first floor, which comprised the owner's apartment, there are mushroom motifs; Calvet loved to gather mushrooms and knew them well. The entrance is also symbolic in design. Next to the cypress adorning the protruding oriel over the entrance, the door-knocker takes the guest by surprise with a particularly pithy motif: the knocker beats on the back of a louse, which stands for evil. In other words, with every knock, the visitor punishes and conquers evil before setting foot in the house.

The design of the interior also holds surprises in store, but these are less conspicuous. The spiralled pillars in front of the staircase look extravagant, but are relatively thin and reserved; they are not made of real granite – even if they look as if they were. On the other hand, the tiled wall of the stairwell is indeed remarkable and contrasts with the pillars. Its bright blue, swirling adornment reminds one of illustrations by William Blake, who as a forerunner of Art Nouveau, had influenced the ornamentational devices which the latter was to employ. It is not so much the overall architectural design which is impressive about this house, even though the two smaller inner courtyards were innovative at the time: Gaudí incorporated them as additional rooms into the house's design by having both lead out directly onto the stairwell. What makes the house intriguing is its "furnishings" in the broad sense of the word. These would include the impressively designed doors, whose large dark brown surfaces provide a restful atmosphere. It would also include small details such as the metal peep-holes, which Gaudí himself designed – he bored his finger into soft plaster and gave the mould to smiths to use as a pattern.

The building stands out from Gaudí's previous works for yet another reason: as in the Güell Palace, he himself designed the furniture for the patron's main living area. Fortunately, the current owner is taking care to preserve not only the house in its original state, but in particular the furnishings. Art Nouveau was the primary influence on Gaudí's furniture designs. At the same time, Gaudí also designed the chairs and seating to fit the general character of the house – plain overall, but imaginative and functional in detail. Compared with the lavishly decorated and overly elaborate furniture of the Güell Palace, these chairs and chairbacks look understated. Occasionally the lines of the backs are interrupted, and the legs are given an elegant sweep downwards. Frequently, large, almost unembellished surfaces create a surprising effect, but look pleasantly flowing and organic, while lacking in even the faintest resemblance to the surface texture of animals or plants.

In this way, the furniture repeats the fundamental characteristic of the house: the interplay of sobriety and a baroque fullness of form, whereby neither of the two ever gains the upper hand.

The Güell Colony Crypt

1898–1917

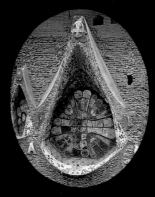

It was originally intended to be a church. A design drawing by Gaudí exists (see opposite), but shows very little detail. Gaudí relied on his own inspiration in the course of its construction. He was full of such ideas — a reason why he did not manage to complete most of his buildings himself. The crypt, however, was left so far from completion that it is necessary to consult his drawing in order to gain even a vague idea of how Gaudí conceived this magnificent work. There are unmistakable similarities with his *magnum opus*, the Sagrada Familia. However, all that one can see at the site today — situated in the middle of the workers' settlement Santa Coloma de Cervelló — is the part, which, in the case of most churches, is usually hidden from view: the crypt. Yet, even this fragment is itself so ingenious that it ranks among Gaudí's masterpieces.

Page 109: Sketch of the outside view of the Güell Colony church. The sketch was based on the picture of a quite unique model: Gaudi had hung little buckshot-filled sacks on strings. The weight of the sacks corresponded (at a ratio of 1:10,000) to the pressure which, according to his calculations, the columns and arches would have to bear. This gave him an inverted model of the entire structure of the building.

Page 111: Hall of columns and entrance to the crypt. The supporting pillars branch out asymmetrically at the top, reflecting the pattern of the branches of the pine trees surrounding the crypt.

Above: Photograph taken in 1913 during the construction work.

It took Gaudí longer and longer to design and carry out his architectural projects, and he gradually deviated from the common practices of an architect — and not only in terms of style. His works since the turn of the century seem to be stations in a continuous process of reflection. The crypt marks the beginning of this development, and it was the only section of what had been planned as a large church to be built. If only for this reason alone, it must be seen in relation to the large-scale project which occupied an increasing amount of Gaudí's time and energy — his work on the Sagrada Familia, where work was then progressing quite swiftly.

Gaudí's friend Güell had set up a textile factory in 1898 and opened a workers' settlement directly adjoining it. It was located south of Barcelona in Santa Coloma de Cervelló. This is why Gaudí's contribution to the settlement has been classified under a variety of names in the relevant literature: as the crypt of the Güell Colony, as the church in Santa Coloma — a somewhat euphoric and all too optimistic characterization, for all that exists of this "church" is the lowermost part, the base of no more than a fragment of the whole building; it is also referred to as the Güell chapel, as the Güell church, or simply Santa Coloma. The multitude of different names is at times a source of confusion.

The original plan did, in fact, call for a church. Gaudí's drawing gives a rough intimation of what it was to look like, but nothing more than that. Rather, Gaudí's drafts for this building, like those of the Sagrada Familia, create more of an overall impression, conveying the desired atmosphere. However, this drawing is not completely without interest, not so much with regard to the church which was planned for the colony, but rather because its style anticipates that of the Sagrada Familia. For example, the church in the drawing is topped by a whole series of towers, such as the admittedly more slender and sharper ones that were later to become part of the Sagrada Familia. It also contains the parabolic arch design, which appeared for the first time in the lobby of the Güell Palace. The lower part of the church follows a horizontal, broadly sweeping, wavy line of the same type

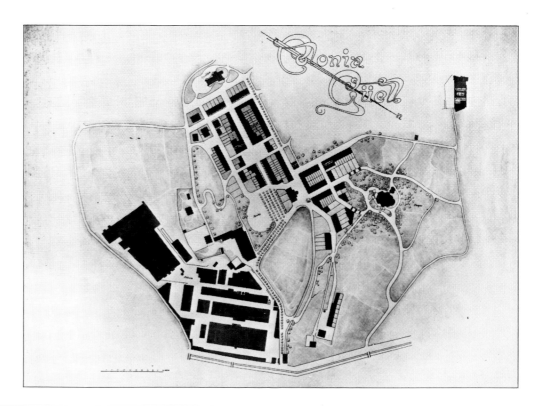

Right: Layout of the Güell Colony.

Pages 112/113: Overall view of the entrance area of the crypt. The hall of columns in front of the crypt looks like a naturally formed cave.

that recurs in the roof of the Sagrada Familia parish school. It also bears similarities, incidentally, to the winding bench in Güell Park. The third basic design component anticipated in the church is a series of slanting pillars used as a foundation; they too recur in Güell Park, which was made at about the same time as the crypt. Both architectural creations belong to one and the same stage of development in Gaudí's design.

It is almost impossible, however, to imagine today how the church was ever to rise up above the crypt. The crypt hugs the upper part of a small hill covered with pine trees, making it inaccessible from behind. In front of the crypt there is a large vestibule supported by pillars. It is difficult to see how these two elements together could serve as the foundation of a large church building. However, Gaudí was always full of surprises, which usually came to light after the fact; it was not until the building was completed that one could see how the individual parts fit together to make a coherent whole, both stylistically and in terms of engineering. In that sense, it is most regrettable that work on the church never got any further, and also that no plaster model was ever made of it; the model made for the Sagrada Familia provided enough information to enable work on the church to proceed, even decades after Gaudí's death.

Be that as it may, Gaudí's work on the crypt of the church could not have proceeded without a model, which, however, was not a model of the finished product, but one that served as a basis for structural calculations. Gaudí worked for more than ten years on this little crypt — a long time, only

Below: Side of the hall of columns, supported by parabolic arches.

warranted if one regards the design plans as a preliminary step in the large scale Sagrada Familia project. Indeed, the crypt provided Gaudí the structural engineer with a field for experimentation, an opportunity to develop the two underlying structural components of his buildings to the full: the already familiar parabolic arch and the slanted pillar. Together with his assistants and colleagues, Gaudí designed a model in which he could assess the respective pressure which would have to be borne by the arches and pillars: he suspended little sacks filled with buckshot from a network of strings, and the sacks corresponded to the respective weights (at a ratio of 1:10,000) which he assumed the arches and pillars would have to support. In this way, the strings formed a structural model of the building, albeit on its head. If the photograph of the model is turned upside down, one can see the structure of the planned building. In other words, Gaudí did not draft a design on the drawing board, but studied the static forces in nature, or at least used a model which replicated the natural ratios.

There is no sign of this in the crypt, of course. Gaudí only studied a model for the project. However, the completed work quite clearly exhibits the results which were achieved by using the model. The pillars are the first thing that catches the eye. Gaudí employed his usual material – bricks, including rounded bricks to some extent, which he arranged to have especially made. This material was complemented with basalt, large pieces of which he put together to form pillars. He then joined the roughly hewn

Grotto next to the hall of columns. Several bent, rounded arches branch off from the supporting columns.

blocks of stone at the seams with lead. When one slowly approaches the centre of the crypt, i.e. the altar, the first reaction is to duck. The pillars slant so sharply that one cannot help thinking that the structure they support will collapse at any moment. Contrary to his usual custom, Gaudí deliberately did not use brick for the central supporting pillars, but large blocks of basalt instead. Perhaps he chose this design to avoid heightening the already fragile sense conveyed by the vaulted ceiling.

However, this chancel is not really a vault. Rather, Gaudí designed the ceiling here, as he did in Bellesguard, with numerous arches masoned in bricks. This makes the room appear lighter toward the top; the ceiling does not seem to bear down so heavily on the columns. The light basalt columns and the brick columns, the bottom third of which are plastered over, enhance this impression. The overall impression is of something that looks less like the product of human hands and more like a cave into which the ceilings have merely been carved, thus making the visitor feel as if he were standing in a large vault. No two elements in the construction are identical. No one pillar is like another, just as no one tree trunk in nature is like another. As a matter of fact, the crypt and Güell Park, which dates from the same period, are the two works by Gaudí which come closest to nature, although he did not by any means attempt to imitate nature. He only incorporated elements already present in it, which of course included structural elements. The stairs leading to the crypt (and originally intended to lead to the entrance of the church per se) reveal the degree to which Gaudí was guided by nature. An age-old pine tree stands on the site of the crypt and other architects would surely have had it felled without a second thought. Gaudí, however, left it where it was and simply ran the stairs

Page 116: Key stone in the hall of columns. Saw and anagram, symbols of the carpenter, are references to St. Joseph.

Page 118: Interior of the crypt. The ceiling is supported by basalt and brick columns.

Below: Magnificently colourful mosaic above the entrance to the crypt

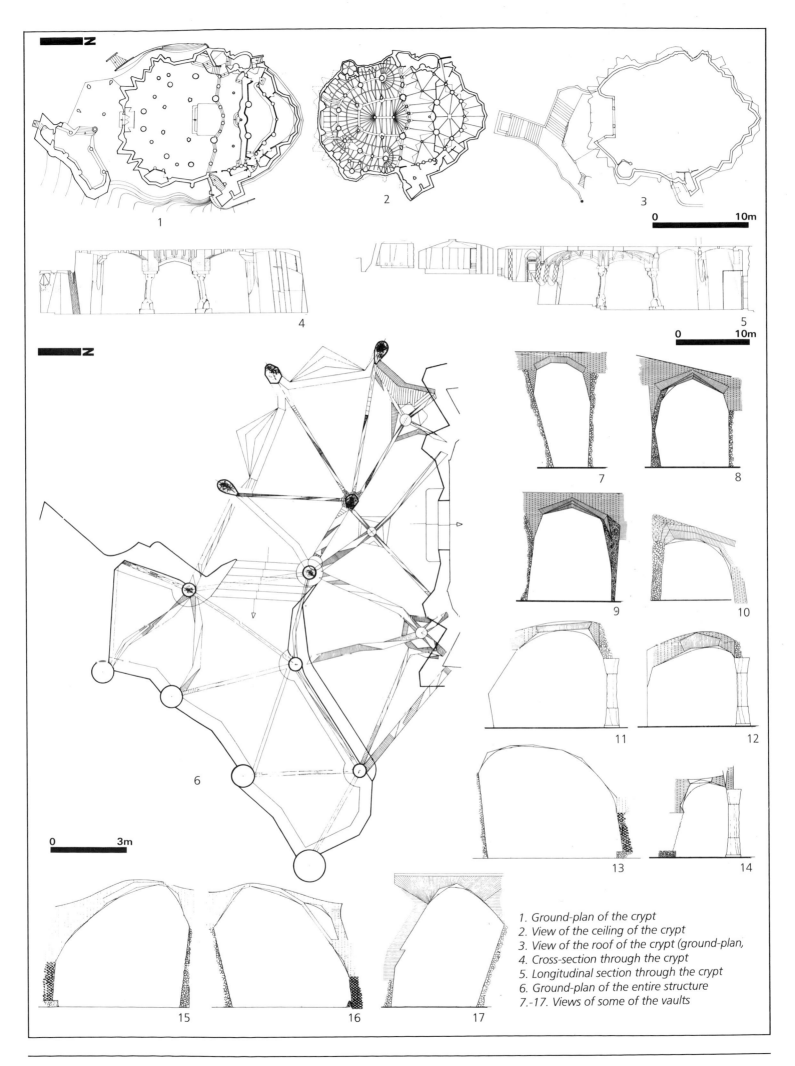

1. Ground-plan of the crypt
2. View of the ceiling of the crypt
3. View of the roof of the crypt (ground-plan,
4. Cross-section through the crypt
5. Longitudinal section through the crypt
6. Ground-plan of the entire structure
7.-17. Views of some of the vaults

Capitals on the slanting supports and struts made of masoned brick (left). Upper part of the supporting column and ceiling ribs (right).

around the tree. It does not take much time to build stairs, he mused, whereas a tree needs much longer to grow. The irregular winding stairs which took shape as a result give the impression of leading around the crypt and enhance the natural aura of the building as a whole.

The chancel itself, which draws the visitor's eyes toward the sacred core (the brick arches meet like spokes in a wheel above the altar) is encircled by a U-shaped hall, which actually contradicts the nature of the crypt. At this point the visitor's gaze is held by a veritable thicket of pillars; unlike the nave of the Sagrada Familia, the pillar design of which resembles a forest, the Güell Colony crypt is marked by irregularity, even primitiveness. Above all, the pillars "branch out" in numerous angles at the top, creating a network of lines. This hall of pillars, which forms the forecourt to the crypt itself, appears to function as a gradual approach to the church. The pillars reflect the structure of a pine forest, a gradual transition from nature to architecture. The architectural principles of the hall of pillars are similar to those used in the crypt, but are all the more obvious to the observer here. This hall, strictly speaking, consists only of oversize (hyperbolical) parabolic arches and slanted walls and/or pillars. They are in themselves sufficient to bear the weight of the vaulted ceiling, which moreover also functions as the foundation for the stairs leading to the main church building. Here the ceiling functions as both ceiling and floor, like the ceiling of the "Greek temple" in Güell Park, which is at once roof and supporting surface for the

market square constructed on top of it. Gaudí thus created a synthesis of supports and weights, which was to attain perfection in the pillars of the Sagrada Familia.

With this crypt design, Gaudí also achieved an ideal combination of a natural-looking exterior and ornamentation – albeit reserved (and understandably so) in comparison with Güell Park. This ornamentation consisted of mosaics which had been created by his colleague Jujol, who also designed the ornaments in the park. Here the affinity with the Sagrada Familia is manifestly evident: the mosaics include two devotional references to Joseph, the patron saint of the Sagrada Familia.

The church of the Güell Colony was never completed. The crypt with the pillared forecourt is but a small torso. And yet here Gaudí created a perfect unity. The gloomy, natural-coloured building hugs the hills and thus, in a way, forms a second, artificial slope. Architecture seems to duplicate nature. This is true all the way down to the details, as in the design of the windows, for example, which are colourful in much the same way as those of Bellesguard, but no longer bear the slightest resemblance to Art Nouveau forms. The crypt windows take forms entirely patterned after nature: they look like coagulated drops of liquid in which the light is colourfully refracted. Even though the crypt may be the first, small part of a large church project, it is nonetheless a perfect, little masterpiece of architecture.

Above: Supporting columns and ceilings inside the crypt (left). Slanting basalt supports (right).

Page 122/123: Outside wall of the crypt with windows. The grating in front of the windows was made of discarded weavers' needles from the Güell Colony factory.

Page 124/125: Stained-glass windows, seen from inside the crypt (above). View of the stained-glass windows from outside (below).

Bellesguard

1900–1909

Gaudí was a Catalonian in every respect. Nearly all
of his works contain small references to his
nationalist convictions. In 1900 he began work on
a structure which became a symbol of Catalonia,
the dream of a great past, a past which lay in the
distant Middle Ages. Gaudí built a country manor
for Doña Maria Sagués which would have been
fitting for a mediaeval prince. The majestic gate,
pointed parapets, and high tower give it the
appearance of a relic from ancient times. Not only
the style is reminiscent of Catalonia's great era,
however, but also the ground on which the manor
was built. This was once the site of a magnificent
country residence — belonging to Martí I, the last
King of Barcelona. Out of a sense of reverence,
Gaudí left the few remains of this old aristocratic
structure untouched — a memorial to the people of
Catalonia.

Gaudí's Catalonian origins and Catalonian patriotism found expression in many of his works. It was not without reason that his friend Joaquim Torres García called him the "most Catalonian of all Catalonians." In the houses he designed (such as the Casa Calvet and the Casa Milà, for example) one repeatedly comes across the words "Fe, Pàtria, Amor", the motto of Jocs Floral, the Catalonian writers' competition. The Catalonian flag with its yellow and red stripes is also a familiar feature, as is the serpent's head of the Catalonian coat of arms (in the form of a large mosaic plate, for example, at the foot of the large staircase at the entrance to Güell Park). In 1907 Gaudí proposed erecting a sun-dial as a monument commemorating the 700th birthday of King Jaume I. And in 1910 he also wanted to dedicate numerous large-scale projects to honour the 100th anniversary of the birth of the Catalonian philosopher Jaume Balmes. Neither of these patriotically inspired projects was carried out, and the government could not be expected to support such a plebeian, and nationalist way of thinking. In the end, Gaudí was only permitted to design two large street lamps in honour of Balmes, and these were removed as early as 1924. After all, Gaudí never did have much luck with public institutions. He carried out his plans and dreams for the most part with the help of private contracts. The Catalonian coat of arms in Güell Park, for example, still exists today.

On the attic floor (below) Gaudí designed the generous ceiling arches out of unfired bricks. On the main floor (extreme bottom) he covered them with a light plaster finish.

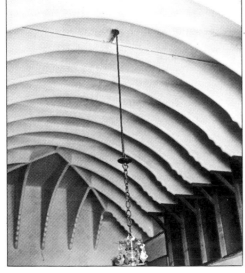

His most patriotic undertaking, however, was the Bellesguard house built between 1900 and 1909. It was built at a time when Gaudí had put his initial, still developmental attempts behind him and struck out on an architectural course of his own, albeit not yet as the mature, completely self-assured architect of the Güell Park.

Viewed purely from the standpoint of architectonic structure, the house is a transitional work. It contains old Gothic elements; the ground-plan is – as in the Casa Calvet – relatively simple. It holds a special position in Gaudí's work as a whole. There are none of the touches of Moorish architecture here, none of the elegant sweeps of his Art Nouveau adaptations, and above all, there is none of the colour which he used to such extravagant effect in Güell Park – where he was also working at the time – and would faithfully employ all the way to the spires of the Sagrada Familia. Even though Bellesguard is not uniform in style – something one never finds in Gaudí's works – it nevertheless has the appearance of a relic of former times. It stands in the landscape like a monolithic block, an impression to which the nearly square ground-plan contributes in no small way.

If it were not for the transversed cross on top of the tower, which can be seen from a distance, and which became almost a trademark of Gaudí's works – then one might think that one is viewing the remains of a mediaeval structure. This was not so very far removed from Gaudí's intentions.

He deliberately alluded to the Middle Ages in designing the building. The house cannot be considered a prime example of Gaudí's new, avant-garde style of architecture; rather, it is a kind of monument to the great Catalonian past. In designing the house, Gaudí drew a great deal of inspiration and guidance from the site on which it was to be built. This was entirely in keeping with the tendencies that he pursued in all his other works during this year. He arranged the overall plan of Güell Park, for example, in line with the natural conditions of the site. In the case of Bellesguard, the building arises out of the historical past of the site. Doña Maria Sagués, the widow of Figueras, had admired the architect for a long time and in 1900 commissioned him to design a building that would revive the historical meaning of the site on which it was to stand: it was here that in 1408 Martí I, the last King of the House of Barcelona, who was known as "the humane one," had had a country residence built. It was he who had coined the name *Bell Esguard* ("beautiful view"), a name of which the house is, incidentally, truly deserving: it is situated half way up the hills that overlook Barcelona and provides a splendid view of the city. Ever since the reign of Martí I, Castile had taken hold of Spain's fate; the golden age of Catalonia had passed.

Page 130/131: Entrance hall and staircase (left). Ventilation duct in the entrance hall and glass windows on a step (right).

Below: Main entrance to Bellesguard with finely executed wrought-iron door.

The windows shaped like pointed arches are another instance of the Neo-Gothic influence. Gaudí toned down the points by adding round elements.

The manor house clearly makes use of mediaeval elements. Here one again encounters the pointed Gothic arches which he had actually already given up using. On one corner, a pointed tower, completely in the style of mediaeval (if not Gothic) palace architecture, soars above the body of this impressive building. However, these are not direct "quotations," but at most vaguely imitated elements. In this way, attention is diverted from the pseudo-Gothic windows to the large cross patterns Gaudí had put below the sills and which repeat the cross which crowns the tower.

The strict design of the façade, which reveals elements of mediaeval castle crenellations, is also reminiscent of the Middle Ages: a sharply-cut parapet encircles the roof like a rampart. The building can be seen as a monument commemorating Catalonia's age of glory – something which Gaudí was not able to get away with in the public spaces of Barcelona. The small mosaics to the right and left of the main entrance can also be interpreted as a symbolic reference to history – two fish in bright blue, and above each of them, a crown – an allusion to Barcelona in former times when it had been the great maritime power. (The "Council of the One Hundred," convened by Jaume I as early as 1259, decreed the *Consolat de Mar,* the first maritime law of modern times, which later probably served as a model for similar constitutions in several Mediterranean states.) The iron entrance gate – as it stands today – does not, however, correspond to Gaudí's intentions. He had designed a wooden gate which fit in better with the austere overall castle design. On the other hand, the iron gate is in tune with the style of the manor. There is none of the elegant ornamentation which Gaudí used in other buildings. Thus, the gate's design is completely in keeping with the window-grating Gaudí created, which, owing to the rounded iron bars (as opposed to the flat iron bands usually preferred) look rigid and uninviting.

But the history of the site was also preserved outside the actual building. Antoni Gaudí left the ruins of the old country manor standing, even attaching them to the newer structure by means of a garden. In order to achieve this, he altered the course of the cemetery path, which originally ran between two tower ruins. For this path he designed a colonnade of slightly slanted pillars – similar to that employed in the Güell Park.

Despite its austere, square shape, the building merges exceptionally well into the landscape. Gaudí combined his favourite material, bricks, with the slate available at the site. As a result, the building has a gloomy look about it, shot through with a fascinating mixture of colours ranging from shades of ochre brown to grey-black. This gloomy impression also predominates on the lower floors. Thick pillars that get wider toward the top, and which, as a result, look somewhat squat and short, support the vaulted ceiling made of brick masonry. The same feature is repeated on the first floor of the attic, but the large hall there is full of light, owing to the large windows. The massive vaulted arches made of brownish, unglazed (i.e. unfired) bricks look almost ornamental, despite the unplastered stone which Antoni Gaudí preferred, true to his style of "honest" architecture that covered up as little as possible.

The upper floors of this building have an amazingly airy ambience, something one would not expect judging from the outside of the house. Gaudí achieved this not only by including a large number of windows, but also and above all by means of an element he had seldom used thus far: the

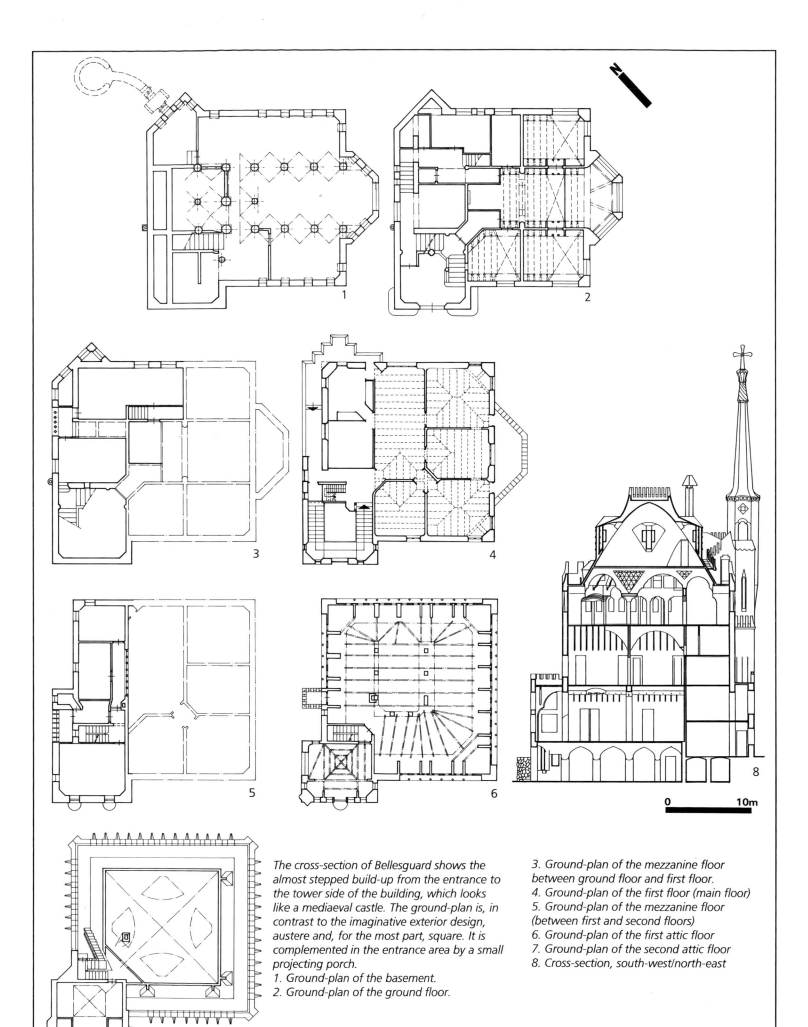

The cross-section of Bellesguard shows the almost stepped build-up from the entrance to the tower side of the building, which looks like a mediaeval castle. The ground-plan is, in contrast to the imaginative exterior design, austere and, for the most part, square. It is complemented in the entrance area by a small projecting porch.
1. Ground-plan of the basement.
2. Ground-plan of the ground floor.

3. Ground-plan of the mezzanine floor between ground floor and first floor.
4. Ground-plan of the first floor (main floor)
5. Ground-plan of the mezzanine floor (between first and second floors)
6. Ground-plan of the first attic floor
7. Ground-plan of the second attic floor
8. Cross-section, south-west/north-east

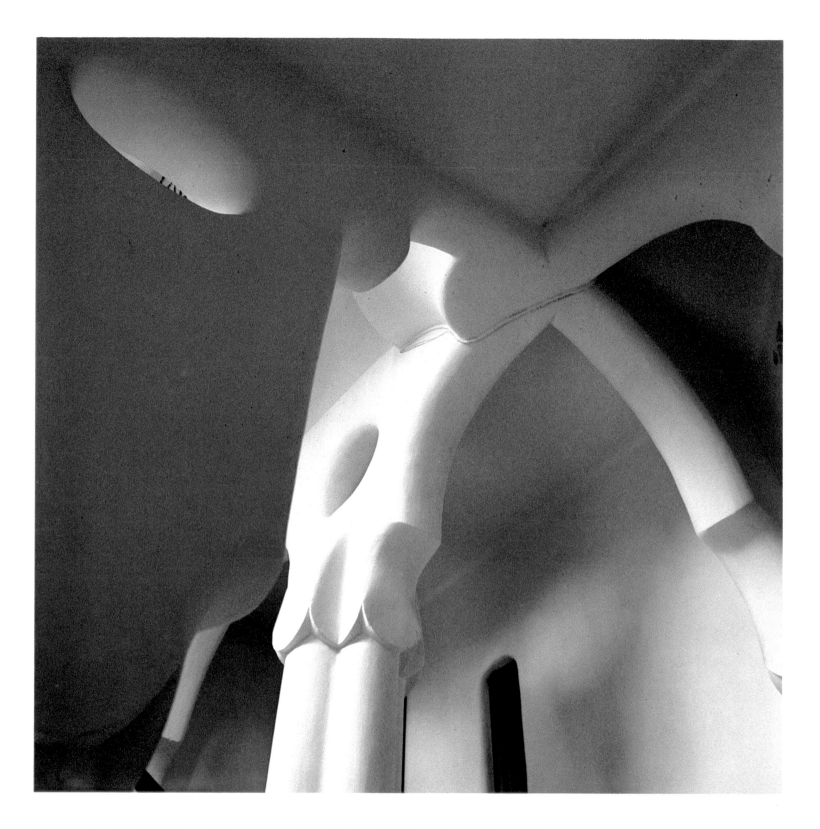

Upper section of a pillar in the ventilation duct. The smooth design from the pillar capital up to the ceiling soaks up the natural light and spreads it throughout the room.

white plaster finish on the walls. In this respect, Bellesguard already anticipated those future works in which light would play an increasingly important role. The plaster finish had still another function: it toned down the room's severe design, making the walls "softer" and the corners less harsh. This is the beginning of the wavy structure used in the Casa Milà. Thus, Bellesguard, which looks so straightforward at first glance, proves to be a complex of contradictions. This is also apparent if one compares the ground-plan and elevation. The ground-plan is almost square; only the front gate protrudes slightly; above it rises the tower (which, by the way, again alludes to the Catalonian coat of arms). The elevation is totally different. The building seems to work upward step by step — a three-tiered

ascent all the way up to the crowning pinnacle, the tower. This gives the castle a certain touch of elegance.

Apart from the basement and the large hall on the first attic floor (which looks extremely complicated, but is in fact simply based on Gaudí's principle of carrying arches), this castle-structure which looks so heavy-set from the outside holds all the elegance of the most beautiful Art Nouveau villa on the inside. The white, almost undulating plaster walls and pillars, which often branch out at odd angles, seemingly leading into other areas and floors, virtually soak up the light, intensify it, pass it on; light and shadow enter into ornamental interplay. One's view does not come to rest anywhere, is forever moved on to something else. This brings us to the

The octagonal convex star in the centre of the glass window is intended to allegorize Venus, the goddess of love.

question of structure. In these white-plastered upper floors, the house appears to be a single room, with numerous bulges and angles. Yet, here again, Gaudí avoids stylistic purity, even when it is a matter of his own style. He used iron bars to support thinner walls. True to his honest nature, he never covered anything up, although it would have been easy for him to do so. Thus, even these rooms, which are so harmonious, always hold surprises in store, "stones that one stumbles over," including even such charming elements as the colourful mosaic windows in which Gaudí playfully alluded to church windows. However, he divided them up into larger complexes reminiscent of Art Nouveau windows, thus embedding symbolic allusions in them — to Venus, the goddess of love. Gaudí combined these Art Nouveau windows, which seem to originate in a different world, with tiled walls in the style of the region. A surprising contrast is in store around the next corner, where the windows are austerely framed in dark wood and gothically pointed toward the top — further evidence that Gaudí was still only playing with the historical elements of style, creating a collage of the most diverse architectural elements. However, his collage never looked like patchwork. Rather, it became a new unity — as did that of the Surrealists later — and, seen as a whole, forms the basis of a new style.

Therefore, the oddly pyramid-shaped roof is not a stylistic flaw either, despite its robust design. If one goes out onto the roof, leaving the ethereally light ambience of the attic's interior, one will see that it is really the crowning feature of the structure, even if it has a playful feel to it: a number of humorous-looking, little pointed window oriels, and especially the "mosaic" of the roof's surface enabled Gaudí to avoid any impression of compact heaviness, which is in fact the building's basic character. The "mosaic" roof surface is only made of undressed stone, but looks astonishingly full of variety and liveliness since Gaudí used the widest variety of stone. Moreover, the roof fits harmoniously into the colour of the landscape. Only the pointed tops of the gallery wall that runs round the roof return us once again to the period which Gaudí wished to invoke with his "Beautiful View" — the Middle Ages, the period in which, in the year 1409, King Martí I married Margarida de Prades at Bellesguard. And it is no coincidence that Gaudí, proud Catalonian that he was, stopped working on this project exactly 500 years after that event, even though he had not completely finished it. Bellesguard is one in a long list of works which Gaudí never finished; it was not until 1917 that Domènec Sugranes completed it.

Above: The parapets, which run like a band around the roof, are reminiscent of mediaeval castles.

Page 136: Interior of the first attic floor (second floor). There is another attic room above this level.

Güell Park

1900 — 1914

Dense pine forests, magnificent avenues lined with palm trees — nowadays, the tract of land in the north-west of Barcelona is indeed what its name promises, namely a park. On the large square surrounded by trees old-age pensioners can be seen chatting and young couples meet for their tête-à-têtes. The coloured bench that leads round the square like some gigantic snake provides generous space for both activities. When Gaudí started work here, however, there was no trace of a park. There were no springs, the land was barren, the slopes bereft of all vegetation. It is Gaudí who must be thanked for the trees and bushes which now grow here. But a straightforward park, a recreational centre for Barcelona's inhabitants, is not what was originally planned. Eusebi Güell, Gaudí's most ardent admirer and sponsor, had intended something that went further: he had planned an exemplary suburban colony, a paradise of homes, a town of gardens. Yet, a park is what emerged — to the benefit of all Barcelona.

Page 139: General view of the main stairs, which fork into two separate flights.

Right: Medallions in mosaic showing the name of the park.

In actual fact, the name of the monumental formation which has taken its place in both Barcelona's landscape and Gaudí biographies — the Güell Park — is an understatement. Admittedly, the area now serves as a municipal park and was planned as such by Eusebi Güell — it was meant to become the second largest park in the city. Güell probably had the idea while travelling abroad; above all, the English landscape gardens had appealed to him, intended as they were to counterbalance the increasing industriali-

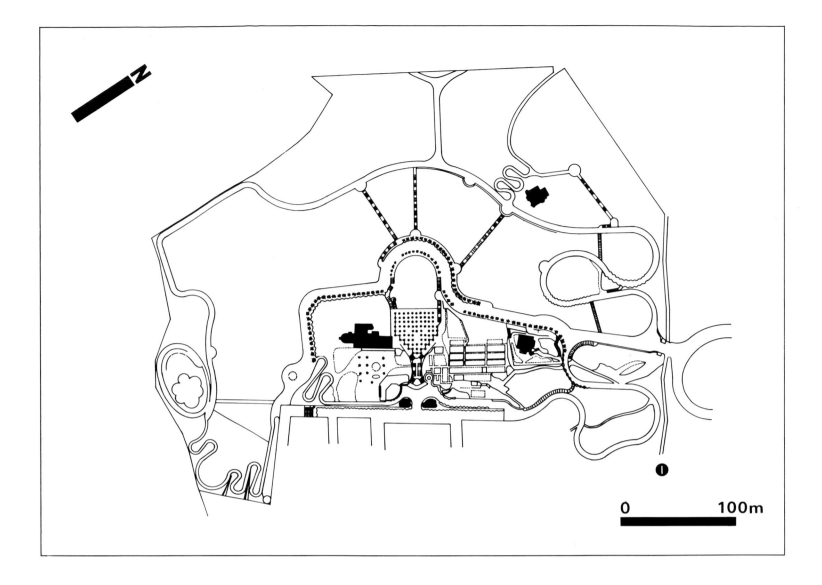

zation of the cities. The example set by the more organic Romantic gardens also most assuredly played a role in the project, with their well-kept ambience that nevertheless bears the stamp of natural vegetation.

This great undertaking can be seen as an extension of the sense of social commitment that had earlier lead Gaudí to collaborate on the project for a workers' settlement in Mataró. Güell devoted much of his attention to the ideas for social reform that were blossoming in the England of the day. (It is clearly no coincidence that Karl Marx was compiling his theoretical works in London at the time.) Güell, at any rate, certainly did not wish to have a private park, even if a perimeter wall was part of the plans from the outset. The latter was meant to give the inhabitants of the area a sense of security, for at the time when it was conceived and built, the park was some distance from the city. Today, the situation has changed. The park was not created to serve as a recreational paradise or as an excursion resort for city-dwellers, but as a suburb, admittedly for persons with somewhat higher aspirations and not exactly without means. 60 triangular allotments were foreseen for this purpose; they were meant to be situated on an expansive, steep slope so that the buildings would not mar the view of the city. All the sites were to be in areas that caught the sun.

The plan failed miserably. Only two allotments were sold and the city showed no interest in the magnificent enterprise. Gaudí himself moved into one of the two houses; not, however, because he wished to live in a

Gaudí planned the large terrace as a place where people could meet and as a square for folk festivals and theatre performances.

stately home — in this respect he was unassuming and became ever more modest the more he immersed himself in his work. In the closing years of his life he even moved into the builders' workshop at the foot of the slowly emerging Sagrada Familia. This was an almost symbolic act, although undertaken purely for practical reasons. Yet, until then it was Güell Park that had been his home. Gaudí thus, in a way, became a neighbour of his great friend, for the old family residence of the Güells was already in the area occupied by the park — the building now houses a school. Gaudí moved into the house because his ninety-three-year-old father, whom he looked after, was no longer able to climb stairs. The architect was already leading the life of a perennial bachelor, caring only for his father and sister's daughter, who lost her mother at an early age. The niece's father was a heavy drinker, unable to guarantee the girl a good upbringing or education. Yet, for all his generosity and good nature, Gaudí could nevertheless be quite a difficult compatriot: he did not, for example, tolerate couples courting in his park.

It is a shame that this magnificent undertaking failed, for Barcelona would have thus brought a settlement model into being that even today would still be pioneering. Gaudí succeeded in his plans in creating a perfect combination of settlement and recreational areas. He had foreseen a sort of "marketplace" at the centre of the site, as a meeting place for the inhabitants and as a venue for theatre and folklore performances.

The "social programme" — mainly Güell's idea — failed, though not that part of the plan for which Gaudí was responsible. Except for two houses,

Two pavilions at the entrance.(left) The office building on the left-hand side of the entrance.(right)

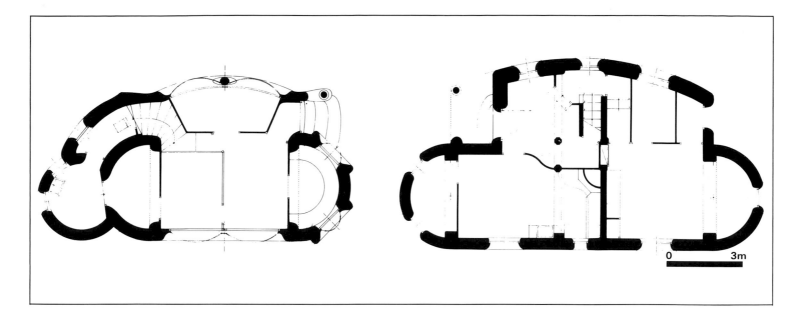

The ground-plan of the porter's lodge and the office building shows how these buildings were "inserted" into the wall surrounding the park.

the area originally intended as a housing estate remained free of buildings. In contrast, the recreational area has blossomed forth as a work of art, a sort of giant three-dimensional monument, as if a sculptor had taken a whole hill as the raw material for a figure. And what a sculptor he was! A man with an unwavering sense of form and colour, a sculptor who at the same time was a painter. Only in the Casa Milà did Gaudí's ability to create sculptures of gigantic proportions take on a more incisive appearance.

As is so often the case in Gaudí's work, the park is comprised of highly differing and mutually exclusive elements. Thus, the eye encounters a wealth of bright, garish colours — which, strictly speaking, should not be part of the overall landscape. Yet, they fit into it harmoniously, enriching it without disturbing. The same impression is left by the infinitely long wall that surrounds the whole park, which totals some 50 acres! The wall really is an alien body, particularly as it is partly coloured. However, it hugs close to every twist and turn in the hilly landscape, merely repeating the contours of the earth.

Here, Gaudí adhered to the principles of English landscape gardening, following the wishes of his employer, Güell, patron of the construction work. And yet his landscape architecture is fundamentally different from the English example on which it was modelled. As was the case with his earlier buildings — which had a sense of the Moorish about them — here Gaudí utilizes only a few of the principles culled from the model, linking them with his own language of forms and thus creating something completely new. The same is true of his Neo-Gothic and Art Nouveau "borrowings".

Güell acquired the Muntanya Pelada — in the northwest of Barcelona — as the land on which to site the park. The land was almost barren of all vegetation — and one could be led to suppose that this would actually provide perfect conditions for a new design. However, the lack of water and the stony, dry earth made the area somewhat unsuitable for a settlement — and in particular for a park with which in the first instance one associates areas of greenery. Gaudí, practically-minded as ever, came up with an ingenious solution to this problem. The land in part slopes steeply, which entailed further problems for construction work. However, this hilly terrain provided the ideal conditions for a winding perimeter wall. Gaudí designed the wall to fit in with the natural environment, but adorned it with strong colours, above all in those places where it would inevitably attract attention, i.e. at the seven entrance gates and especially at the main entrance. Here, in the Calle Olot, the lower part of the wall – roughly two-thirds of it in terms of height – is built of ochreous undressed stone. Towards its crest, the wall gets thicker and is topped with a winding cover, composed of a mosaic of white and brown ceramic tiles. This has a number of advantages. Firstly, the wall covering is very decorative; in bright sun-light the wall gleams. Gaudí, however, also had some very practical inten-tions with this construction. What was actually inferior material would have been subject to the erosion of rain had it not been protected, but because of the "ceramic skin" the walls are water-proof. At the same time, Gaudí also strengthened the wall's function as protection against intruders from outside: the rounded-off, smooth covering offers the fingers no purchase. The wall can only be scaled with great difficulty if aids are not used. Indeed, the park as a whole is a unique synthesis of practical purposes and aesthetic effect. It demonstrates Gaudí's twofold talents perhaps even more clearly than do his other works.

The main entrance was designed solely in terms of aesthetic criteria. It is flanked by two pavilions that at first sight resemble houses from some magical forest. The walls seem to be irregular and look as though they have only been fused together into a house with the greatest difficulty – and the roof undulates irregularly. And yet, as elsewhere, this lack of uniformity is misleading. Pavilions and wall do indeed form a unit. The pavilions have an

Page 147: A terrifying dragon with "scales" of small coloured tiles guards the park. He represents Python, the guardian of the subterranean waters.

Page 149: Columned hall. The roof, which simultaneously serves as the floor for the Greek theatre, is borne by Doric columns.

oval ground-plan; their walls appear to grow out of the park's wall, or put differently, the pavilions resemble "insertions" into the great perimeter wall. These small houses are, like the wall, both built of ochreous undressed stone, and rendered in a similarly colourful structure of gleaming tiles. Only the 30-foot high turret on one of the two pavilions stands out against its background. It is without function – like the tower of El Capricho – and encased in a checkerboard-like pattern of small blue and white tiled squares. Yet again, the observer would seem to be confronted by a contradiction, a breach of the landscape's harmony, but here Gaudí incorporated the colours of the background as they must appear to the passer-by on the street: the blue of the sky and the white of clouds floating by. Just as in the wall, small medallions are embedded in the pavilions with the name of the park on them: ornamental trifles, but each with a meaningful function.

The entrance area already points to the main construction principles that the visitor will then encounter throughout the park: dumbfounding effects that attract the eye as if by magic and yet embedded in a harmony that fuses everything into one unit. The impression is of expensive, brightly gleaming materials – in what is nevertheless a construction using the cheapest of raw materials. The park was almost completely built of material that was found on the actual site, and quite a lot was found indeed. The terrain was too steep for roads and paths. Gaudí decided not to have parts of the hill levelled; he wanted to subject his architecture utterly to the

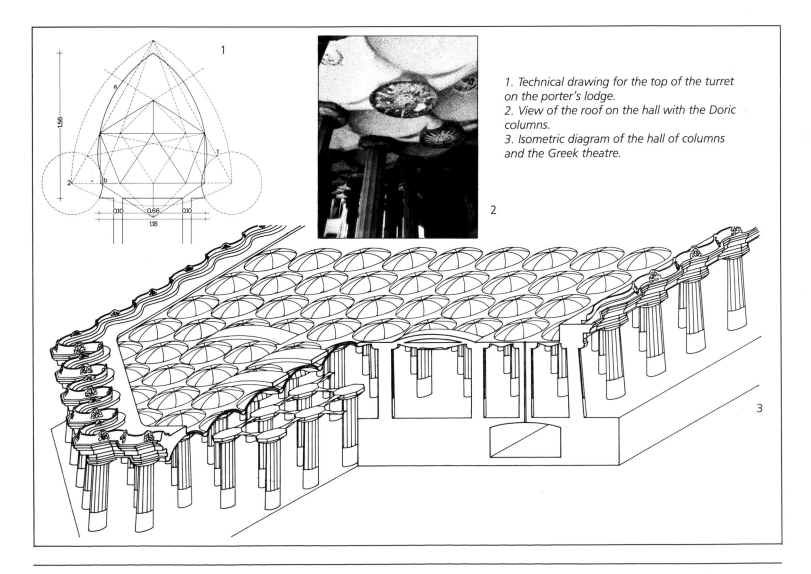

1. Technical drawing for the top of the turret on the porter's lodge.
2. View of the roof on the hall with the Doric columns.
3. Isometric diagram of the hall of columns and the Greek theatre.

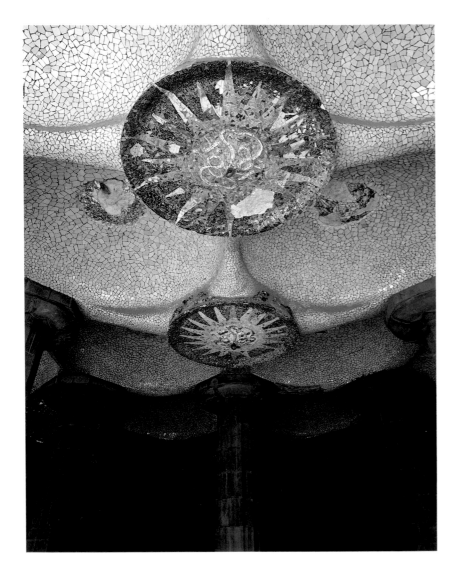

Mosaic medallions by Josep M. Jujol adorn the ceilings of the hall of columns.

dictates of the existing landscape. He thus designed the streets in the form of viaducts and caverned passages. In this manner he obtained stone materials, rubble, from which he then constructed his buildings. The splendid, gleaming ceramic coverings were composed by means of a collage, the *trencadis:* he procured waste, rejects, slivers and chips from good ceramic workshops which were then pressed into the mortar while this was still soft. Thus, at the beginning of the century he already preempted an art movement that was to first blossom forth in the '20s: the collage technique of the Dadaists. If it had not been for the work of his collaborator, Josep Maria Jujol, who was a specialist in such ceramic artworks, the overall construction might have been less sumptuous and luxurious. However, such speculations are rather pointless: architecture does not occur without collaboration, and Gaudí in particular was an ardent proponent of collective projects. Work, he once said, was the fruit of cooperation, and the latter was only possible on the basis of love. By dint of his continual presence at the construction site of the Sagrada Familia he put this theory into practice.

Gaudí was never a pure theoretician. It was his conviction that the architect's task was not to invent giant projects, but rather to make these possible. Such a view clearly accords with the great 19th century tradition of architecture. The last decades of that century saw the dissemination of a wide-ranging pragmatism, particularly in England, where the most popular

manifestation was to be found in the work of William Morris. Morris thought of himself mainly as an artist, but was in fact a furniture manufacturer – inspired moreover by thoughts of social reform As a consequence, Morris repeatedly attempted to design pieces of furniture of an aesthetically high standard and in such a manner that the ordinary man on the street, indeed even the working-class man, could afford them. The intention was to upgrade everyday life aesthetically. Morris would most surely have been pleased by the basic idea underlying Güell Park. Gaudí, in other words, embarked on his career at a time when people were bent on overcoming the division between art and crafts, and by extension, between art and life. Güell Park is concrete proof that this idea is not only correct, but can be put into practice. The fact that the city was not enthusiastic about the project also shows, however, that the public was far from ready to receive such progressive ideas. (In our age of mass production, a distance is again growing between the two areas of art and craft.)

Gaudí, with his use of trivial, and indeed pathetic means to achieve great aesthetic effects, anticipated the ideas that brought the Cubists, particularly his compatriots Picasso and Miró, worldwide success. The utilization of materials that were of an inferior quality and thus less durable, however, posed great constructional problems for Gaudí, so that he had to construct his buildings as complex structures with many different layers in order to ensure their durability. Nevertheless, from the outside they appear to have been moulded in one piece. For example, the superstructure of turrets on the pavilion is hollow. The walls are made up of a 2½" thick inner layer of bricks and a layer of concrete, reinforced with ten millimetre-thick iron rods; this was the first time Gaudí had used such a material. This is then covered by three layers of roofing tiles and finally by an external coat of cement in which the ceramic plates are embedded, forming the mosaic.

The whole park is constructed in a similarly ingenious manner. The form of construction – invisible to the eye – first became apparent when the city of Barcelona, which has owned the park since 1922, carried out renovation work. Such work was, incidentally, not necessary until a surprisingly late date; a hallmark of Gaudí's buildings is that they are incredibly durable, even if they look as fragile as the neat small ornamental turrets on the roofs.

What is fascinating above all is the architectonic design of that part of Güell Park which was not intended as a housing area and which thus exhibits the real quality of a park as a living space. Once the visitor has gone through the entrance, flanked on either side by the two pavilions, he is faced by a monumental flight of outdoor stairs that reminds him of the great castles of yesteryear. He can go up two parallel sets of stairs – separated from one another by a large bed of organic sculptures in stone and bordered by a low stone wall – to the central sector of the park, a sector that, were he standing at the foot of the stairs, one would not even imagine existed. Before reaching this sector, the visitor's path is blocked by a monster – in a sense, the last guardian of the park: a huge dragon

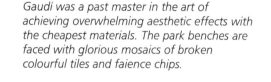

Gaudí was a past master in the art of achieving overwhelming aesthetic effects with the cheapest materials. The park benches are faced with glorious mosaics of broken colourful tiles and faience chips.

covered in bright "scales" of small tiles. People acquainted with Gaudí's work are already familiar with this creature. A similar animal was already to be encountered on the Güell estate, admittedly in the form of a playful, Art-Nouveau wrought-iron gate. As is always the case in Gaudí's later work, one must suspect a deeper, usually symbolic meaning lurking behind everything that appears to be playful on the surface. The dragon represents Python, guardian of the subterranean waters, and Gaudí thus alludes darkly to what is of immense importance for the park, but which escapes the eye: behind the dragon a cistern lies concealed that can contain up to 2,600 gallons of water; it was conceived of as a rainwater collector. In this manner, rainwater was channelled into the collector and stored to irrigate the barren parkland, deprived as it is of any natural springs.

A few yards further on, one meets yet another reptile – a snake's head – which also serves a symbolic purpose. Gaudí alludes here to the Catalonian coat-of-arms: a snake's head against yellow and red lines. And, practical-minded as ever, Gaudí at the same time used both reptiles as overflow valves for the cistern.

The flight of stairs itself reminds the visitor of centuries past; yet, if he goes up it, he feels as if he were transposed into an even more distant past. An ochre-coloured hall of columns rises up like a Greek temple. The columns are – with slight differences – Doric in form. Perhaps Gaudí wanted to pay homage to his financial sponsor's enthusiasm for Classical Antiquity. The pillars are arranged in such a manner that they appear to stand at the intersecting points of an imaginary net. Depending on where

Pages 154 - 157: Details from the park bench mosaics. A part of the pattern for the mosaics was devised by Gaudi himself, the remainder created collectively by the workers engaged in building the park. Both symmetrical patterns and irregular, fantastic decorations emerged from this use of the diverse shapes of faience chips and ceramic fragments.

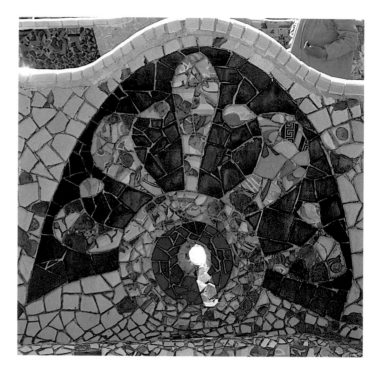

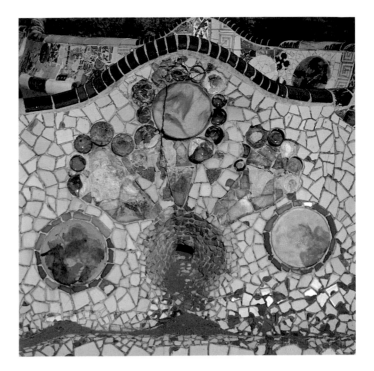

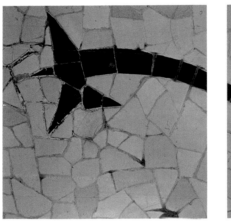

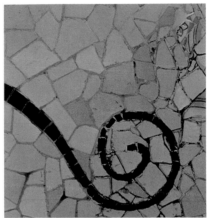

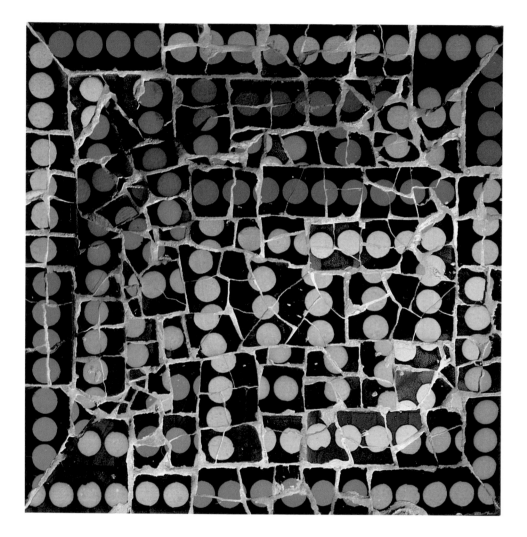

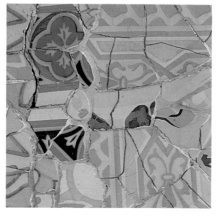

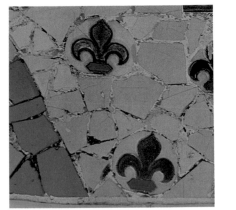

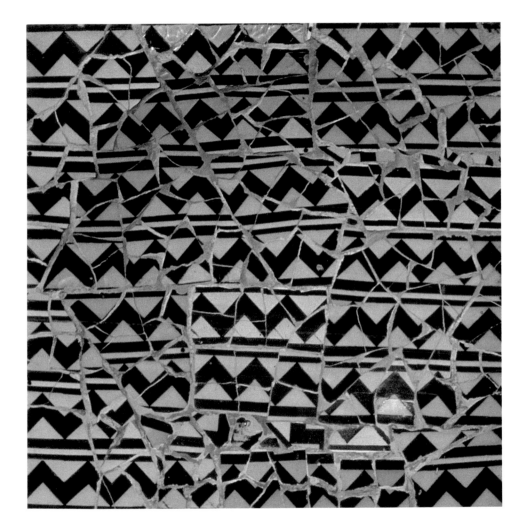

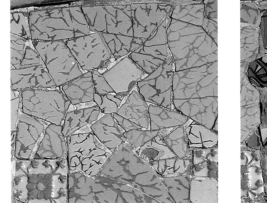

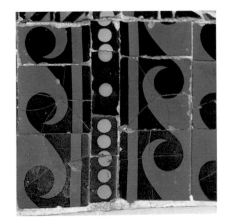

the observer stands, the columns appear to form an impenetrable forest of columns or a structure comprising several rows of columns, in which all the subsequent pillars disappear behind the first row. Gaudí would, however, not have remained true to himself had he not also had some fun while designing this memorial to Classical Greece. The outside columns are – true to Greek custom – slightly oblique and broaden slightly towards the base. However, in Gaudí's work these features are a bit more exaggerated than in the original Doric columns. The remaining pillars in the interior of the "hall" are all of the same size. The architectonic elements of the park always have several functions. Just as the two reptiles are ornament, symbolic allusion and overflow valves all at once so too the columns are not just pillars supporting a roof, and the roof is not just a roof but the floor of something else. Indeed, it would seem that the function as a roof is only secondary, for the outer side of the roof serves as the square at the centre of the whole park. This space was intended as the "market-place" for the settlement and – also following the example of Antiquity – at the same time as the site for a theatre. The whole park as it was originally planned can thus be thought of as one gigantic amphitheatre. The "audience" would not have sat in rows directly surrounding the stage, however, as these "rows" are to be found on the slope opposite the square; the "seats" would have been the settlement houses themselves. What remains of this plan is the square – without the settlement. This "Greek theatre", as Gaudí was fond of calling the square, is of quite awe-inspiring proportions: 258 x 120 feet. Only approximately half of it is built on solid ground; the other half rests on the Doric columns. Thus, the Greek hall of columns is actually only the foundations of the immensely larger Greek theatre. The pillars serve in this context not just to support the roof, but at the same time as water conduits for rainwater. Such an open space collects a large quantity of water in a relatively short period of time. The columns, as compact as they may appear, are hollow; and the floor of the Greek theatre conceals a highly complex internal network. It is absolutely flat, not inclining in any direction; as a result the water does not flow in one single direction. Gaudí developed this drainage system by copying nature, something he did frequently in his mature phase. The floor of the square is not cemented; the water can thus seep into the ground, where it enters one of innumerable collecting vessels; these resemble pipes split down the middle with small openings underneath from which the water can flow into the hollow pillars. The fact that the water is also filtered during its journey into the cistern shows just how much detailed scrutiny the architect put into the design of his buildings. Small wonder that when the City of Barcelona awarded him a prize for the Casa Calvet, it was not just for the high aesthetic standard of the building, but also for his achievements in the field of ventilation and de-aeration as well as sewage removal. The symmetrical lay-out of the columns was, incidentally, interrupted in a few places, so that the hall did not appear over-cluttered. In the spaces that thus remained "free" his collaborator, Jujol, installed some fascinating, large-scale medallion-like decorations.

This by no means exhausts the wealth of different functions fulfilled by this building complex. The wall surrounding the square not only serves to prevent inquisitive passers-by from falling down the steep slope, but was also designed as one long bench. The terrace thus also became a place to

Below and page 159: Gaudí followed the dictates of nature in designing the paths and roads. Instead of levelling hills he created a number of cavernous passageways formed by oblique supporting walls and pillars.

meet people, especially as this "endless bench" did not follow any clear, sober line. It winds its way in innumerable and highly differing curves round the giant terrace. In this way it offers seating space for many people and it is, above all, structured in such a manner that the people — although outdoors and in large number — can nevertheless form small intimate groups in which to have a chat, as it were. It is a "chance" side-effect that an organic form is thus also bestowed on the wall bench. In this phase of his work Gaudí attached greatest importance to an organic method of building. He accordingly took great pains when designing the bench to ensure that the seating and back of the bench accorded with the physiology of the human body. In order to reproduce the form of the body with the greatest precision he is said to have sat a naked man on plaster that was still pliable, and then reproduced the imprint at a later stage. However abstract the ornaments on the bench may be, they are nevertheless – as is so much of Gaudí's architecture – close to reality, "human", "natural". To ensure that one's sense for colour did not go unheeded, he applied here what is perhaps the most opulent and artistic utilization of "broken ceramics". Using thousands of broken, coloured tiles and pieces of faience, he had a mosaic created on the bench which greatly excels the decor of the roofs and walls. He relied in this context on his workers' artistic sensibilities. He could never have designed and distributed all the parts of the mosaic himself. One critic believes there is proof that the bench was decorated from right to left; if one moves in this direction, he says, one can observe an ever-increasing degree of artistic workmanship and imagination. Gaudí, as it were, created with this collective project a picture by Miró before the latter had even started painting. (The work on the park lasted from 1900 to 1914; Miró was born in 1893.) At the same time, the bench is both waterproof and extremely hygienic owing to the coat of mosaics.

As rich in colour as the bench is, it nevertheless does not appear out of place perhaps precisely because of its organic twists and turns which – like the park's perimeter wall – reproduce the contours of the hill. The network of roads in the park is characterized by a similar harmony with nature. If the bench is Gaudí's great accomplishment in terms of surface design, then the network of roads is his great achievement in the area of construction and structural engineering. He later based his deliberations when building the

Two-storied promenade (left). Promenade with slanting, spiralled columns (right).

Sagrada Familia on these findings. In order to avoid any levelling of the terrain, he planned the roads in twists and turns – they run close to the edge of the incline and repeatedly pass under colonades – as well as making use of constructions that appeared completely natural. He had the pillars made of brick as this caused only a minor optical disruption of the natural landscape. These colonades often form caverns that seem to have evolved naturally. The slanting pillars have proved to be very sturdy, irrespective of how fragile they may appear to be. Gaudí had, after all, conducted intensive tests with models. At the same time, they provide shelter from the rain and over-bright sunlight and are outfitted with benches that were built into the stone. Wherever possible, if nature preordained a certain form, then this was adopted in the architecture.

With Güell Park, Gaudí designed a settlement in what was until then uninhabited terrain and at the same time paid such a great deal of attention to preserving the natural landscape that the result could serve as a model in our times. Indeed, in 1984 the park was placed under an international preservation order by UNESCO. Architecture and nature enter a unique alliance in the Güell Park project: the architecture not only conforms to the landscape – it appears to have grown out of it. At first sight one frequently takes a pillar that ends at the top in a flower tub to be a palm tree. (And one can make the opposite mistake.)

What distinguishes Güell Park from all Gaudí's buildings is that it exhibits the greatest proximity to nature. From this point of view the architect then created his later buildings: these placed a second, new nature alongside first nature.

The highest point of the promenade. The struts bearing the wall serve as flower tubs at the top. They are a particularly impressive example of how Gaudí imitated forms from nature in his work.

Casa Batlló

1904 – 1906

Mighty pillars that appear to resemble the feet of some giant elephant are the first thing to meet the eye of the passerby from street level. The roof reminds him of a completely different animal: it is bordered by a jagged line similar to the backbone of a gigantic dinosaur. A façade extends between the two, including a number of small, elegantly curved balconies that seem to stick to the front of the house like birds' nests on the face of a cliff. The façade itself glitters in numerous colours, and small round plates that look like fish scales are let into it. There are no edges or corners here; even the walls are rounded in undulations and have in essence the feel of the smooth skin of a sea serpent about them. Salvador Dalí praised Gaudí for his "soft calf-skin doors". In the Casa Batlló even the outer walls appear to be made of leather, soft and supple. This dream of softness and naturalness is then continued inside the building.

Page 163: The outer façade, ornamented with pieces of mosaic and ceramic tiles, seems to move in the morning sunlight as if to the rhythm of the sea.

There is probably no other building that better illustrates what is modern in Gaudí's work and that does so in such a sensuous, almost symbolic manner than this second and last of his apartment house projects. As so often, he was not able to start from scratch with the Casa Batlló, but was tied to an already existing building shell. In the case of the Colegio Teresiano this had led him to introduce his conception of what the main elements of a house should be via a small number of substantial changes to the construction – impressing his mark on the house with but a few artistic tricks.

This is not the case in the narrow house in 43, Passeig de Gràcia. When viewing the building today, it defies one's imagination to conceive what it once looked like. A comparison of the basic outline with the front elevation gives us an idea, however. Josep Batlló i Casanovas, a wealthy textile manufacturer, wished to completely change the appearance of his existing residence in this fashionable district of Barcelona. The apartment block had been built in 1877 and is said to have been one of the most boring and conventional houses in the district. A large number of modern buildings had arisen in the immediate vicinity. Batlló clearly wanted to outdo these buildings in terms of modernity, for Gaudí's obstinate originality in architectural design was already well-known. Pere Milà, a friend of Battló's, brought the two men into personal contact, but Battló is sure to have been known to the textile manufacturer. The spectacular buildings undertaken for Güell – the palace not so far away from the Passeig de Gràcia, and Güell Park, which was taking shape at the time – had made Gaudí into a celebrity. And the size of the project Batlló probably had in mind can be gathered from the fact that in 1901 he applied to Barcelona's municipal

Below: Original sketch by Gaudí of the façade in the suggestive style so typical of his late phase.

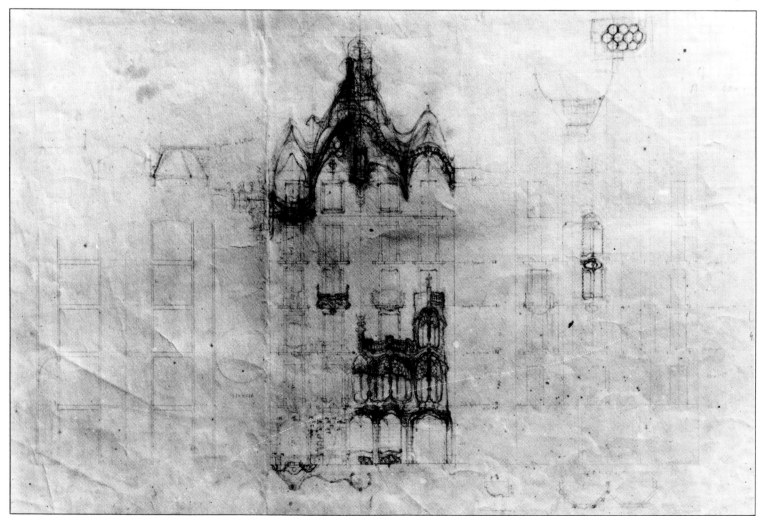

authorities to have the old building torn down in order to erect a completely new one. However, things did not go quite that far, perhaps because Gaudí did not need such a radical break with the old. To create an utterly new building by means of but a few incisive alterations was not without its challenges. And, indeed, the building that emerged was completely new, even in terms of Gaudí's own work.

This feeling can be sensed even at the bottom of the building, which was originally very narrow at the base, but was made to seem of enormous dimensions. Gaudí's work was forever affected by the limited space of the construction sites: although his buildings all appear magnificent, they are nevertheless anything but large. With a few artistic tricks Gaudí always created an illusion of magnitude. The giant iron gates achieve this for the Güell Palace. In the rebuilding of the Batlló house it was the thick pillars that he used to this end; they form an arcade around the entrance and their thickness gives the impression that the house must be of truly gigantic proportions. These pillars immediately sparked off a conflict between Gaudí and the municipal authorities. There had been objections raised by the authorities with respect to the Casa Calvet. Whereas in the latter case the bone of contention had been the height, which exceeded the permitted limits, here it was the width. The pillars jutted out a full two feet over the pavement. The pedestrians quite literally stumbled over the house – in a metaphorical sense as well. Seldom did Gaudí cause such a stir with a building as in the case of the avant-garde architecture used here. But, as with the Casa Calvet, Gaudí obviously ignored the objections raised by the

The platform on the main building (first floor). Natural Montjuïc stone was polished in such a manner that rounded surfaces emerged which created the impression of a moulded clay sculpture.

Above: The ground and first floor façades (left). Ventilation tract in the inner courtyard. The colours that grow softer as they progress down the building and the different sizes of the windows take account of the amount of light which is cast into the courtyard.

Page 167: Entrance hall and stairwell.

Pages 168/169: A striking example of Gaudí's design of the rooms: The ceilings and walls seem to have been modelled – there are no straight lines or smooth surfaces.

authorities. The pillars, after all, are still standing. And the second attack by the civil servants also went unheeded. Inside the building he had installed a mezzanine floor, and in the attic two rooms had been constructed that had not been entered on the original application for building permission. What at first sight would seem to be some formalistic argument between architect and authorities does, however, go to the very heart of Gaudí's approach. His buildings emerged in the course of construction work. This procedure assumed gigantic proportions, after all, in the case of the Sagrada Familia, yet as early as the Güell Colony Crypt unusual dimensions had arisen. Perhaps Gaudí had envisaged problems with the authorities and had thus submitted a sketch that was rich in atmosphere but said nothing about the construction at hand. But meanwhile this had become his planning method. Free-hand drawings were also all the plans that were used for the Crypt and the Sagrada Familia; all three are in fact quite similar.

And yet at the beginning of the construction work Gaudí had nothing to hide. The full extent of his version of the avant-garde did not reveal itself until the final stages. If one compares the building plans for the old house and the end product, then it soon becomes obvious that Gaudí actually abided quite strictly by the plan. The old house consisted, on the whole, of right-angled structures: the ground-plan is repeated on each floor and the façade is dominated by four long, right-angled windows per floor. Gaudí took up this distribution of the windows, simply redesigned the forms and covered panels of the windows from scratch and supplemented these with

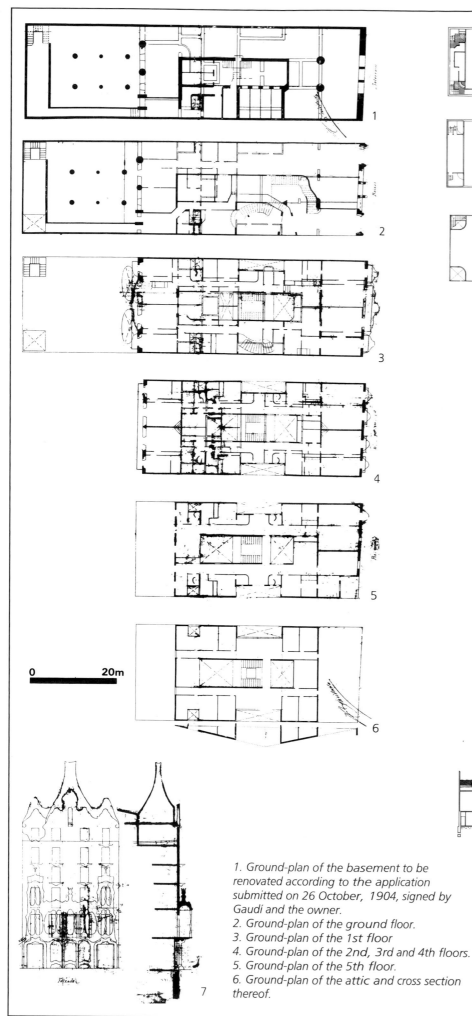

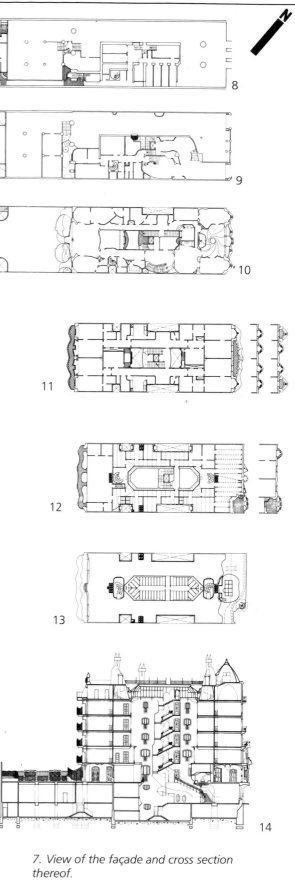

1. Ground-plan of the basement to be renovated according to the application submitted on 26 October, 1904, signed by Gaudí and the owner.
2. Ground-plan of the ground floor.
3. Ground-plan of the 1st floor
4. Ground-plan of the 2nd, 3rd and 4th floors.
5. Ground-plan of the 5th floor.
6. Ground-plan of the attic and cross section thereof.

7. View of the façade and cross section thereof.
8. Ground-plan of the ground floor.
9. Ground-plan of the basement.
10. Ground-plan of the 1st floor.
11. Ground-plan of the 2nd, 3rd and 4th floors.
12. Ground-plan of the 5th floor.
13. Ground-plan of the attic.
14. Longitudinal section of the whole building.

bizarre-shaped little balconies which seem to stick to the window-sills like little drops of hardened honey – and with that, a completely new type of house had come into being.

The cast-iron railings – that had themselves served as the complete balcony in earlier buildings – are supplemented, engulfed and flattered by softly undulating elements of walling and plaster. There are no corners or straight lines whatsoever, as if everything were in fluid motion. And it is above all the façade as a whole that has such an effect, as if Gaudí had completely renounced the use of traditional building materials. Bricks, the material for which he had until then shown a preference, are not even used as ornaments in Casa Batlló, although this was a technique Gaudí commanded perfectly. The façade is coated in flat Montjuïc stone with the sandstone colours that have a feel of modelled clay about them – a feature emphasized by the manner in which the surface has been worked. Gaudí gave everything a wavy, undulating shape. The house has more the appearance of a gingerbread house than one made of stone. The mosaics in the façade complete this sense of standing before a magician's home. The number of ceramic components used increases towards the roof. The roof itself is covered in bluish-pink tiles on the side facing the street. The crest of the roof runs in an undulating line that traces a slight zig-zag on account of the round tiles used.

The entire house seems to be the brainchild of someone whose mind has detached itself from everything that hitherto existed and who follows only its own dreams and visions. And yet Gaudí, as was the case with many of his previous buildings, paid great attention to the surroundings of the house. The zig-zag of the roof, for example, corresponds with the strict, stepped gable of the house to the left. Gaudí also took the neighbourhood into account when deciding on the Casa Batlló's height, foregoing a fully-fledged attic. In this manner the house gradually tapers toward the roof, which thus becomes a hat or a hood with a delightful little ornamental turret on one side – like a feather in a cap. This small turret is crowned by what had become Gaudí's trademark, namely the horizontal cross.

The playful impression is continued in the house's interior. Gaudí concentrated on the rooms that were going to be occupied by the owner of the building. These could not be more remote from conventional rooms. Gaudí merged everything with everything else. He had tried to do this in places in the Güell Palace, but it was not until the Casa Batlló that he succeeded in completely overcoming the usual division between rooms.

Although Gaudí followed a path of his own, it has been suggested that there are links here to Art Nouveau. But irrespective of the imaginative design of these rooms, they are based on a surprisingly sober structural principle. The ground-plan and façade of the old house were based on a rectangular structure. In Gaudí's building these also accord with one another, the sole difference being that the underlying forms are completely new. Just as the windows look like outgrowths of plants, not one of them identical with another, so too the ground-plan is determined by irregular forms. It resembles above all the "construction plan" of organic cells.

Pages 174, 175: Two examples of Gaudí's imaginative roof design. Spherical and cylindrical ceramic tiles are used alternately on the crest of the water tank to the left, ; the crest thus seems to be the back of a fearsome dragon or dinosaur (Page 174). Gaudí decorated the ventilation stacks and chimney pots with fragments of tiles (page 175).

Below: The door leading to the main first floor (left). Doors dividing the rooms on the main first floor between the hall and the study (right).

Casa Milà

1906 – 1910

La Pedrera – "the quarry" – was the name an
astounded population gave to this completely
unique building. It could be compared with the
steep cliff walls in which African tribes build their
cave-like dwellings. The wavy façade, with its large
pores, reminds one also of an undulating beach of
fine sand, formed, for example, by a receding
dune. The honeycombs made by industrious bees
might also spring to the mind of the observer
viewing the snake-like ups-and-downs that run
through the whole building. In this last secular
building which he constructed before devoting all
his energies to the Sagrada Familia, Gaudí created
a paradox: an artificial but natural building which
was simultaneously a summary of all the forms
that he has since become famous for. The roof
sports an imitation of the bench from Güell Park as
well as an ever more impressive series of bizarre
chimney stacks.

Page 177: Limestone was used for the façade. Originally, the stone had a creamy colour which has changed as a result of air pollution.

Page 180/181: Overall view of the façade of this forceful corner house.

Below: A mighty column rests on the pavement like an elephant's foot.

With the Casa Batlló, Gaudí had actually reached the zenith of his design of secular buildings. One can hardly conceive of a greater freedom, a more magnificent and anarchic development of imaginative forms that nevertheless relies on traditional house forms. What is more, in the Casa Batlló Gaudí had perfected this new stylistic phase. In Güell Park and the Güell Colony Crypt he had approximated nature to such an extent that the buildings seemed to resemble a second nature, an artistic redesigning of nature's forms and construction principles. And he sublimated this approach in the Casa Batlló. Pure art forms reminiscent of nothing but nature evolved from these near-natural forms. There is a great deal of truth in it when the façade is compared with the surface of a sea whipped up by a storm. The small splinters of mosaic in the façade remind one of the foaming crests of the waves; yet, under Gaudí's hand these become purely ornamental elements. Gaudí did not make forms in order to copy nature. Even the furniture that he created for the house owner was unmistakably fashioned after the human body — but Gaudí did not use any anatomical forms. The days were over when he would shape door-handles in such a way that they could be taken for bones. His intensive preoccupation with nature had allowed him to assimilate its essential underlying structures: he could now play with them at will, as he did with the existing architectural styles when he first started design work. He also played with elements of his own style, which became ever clearer in this, the mature phase of his art.

With regard to the wealth of imaginative ideas, the Casa Batlló is certainly not outclassed by the Casa Milà. The fascinating use of colour is missing, as is the sumptuous use of different ceramic materials and forms. And one could search in vain in the interior of this last house designed by Gaudí for the staircase that brings to mind the over-sized backbone — perhaps of a dinosaur — a motif repeated on the ridge of the roof. In this respect, Gaudí had already reached the pinnacle of his achievements. It is difficult to say why he nevertheless took on the job that his friend Pere Milà offered. Perhaps it was the dimensions involved that tickled his fancy. At long last he did not need to create an illusion of largeness for a building, but was able from the very outset to build on a grand scale. The building was sited only a few houses away from the Casa Batlló, on the corner of the Passeig de Gràcia and the Calle de Provença. Gaudí had to depart from the structure he had adopted in earlier buildings as he now had to work with a corner-house. Previously he had emphasized the entrance way, either by means of a balcony-platform as in the Güell Palace, or a richly decorated oriel as in the Casa Calvet or the linking of balcony-platform and an archway in the Casa Batlló. Needless to say, in the Casa Milà, which was to serve as a large apartment block, several entrance ways were required. Indeed, Gaudí originally planned a wide ramp for one of the two large courtyards so that even coaches could drive right up to the door; he later deviated from this plan however.

The surface area, over 10,000 square feet in size, posed a challenge. With a special design for the corner façade Gaudí gave the house the character of a detached building, although it was flanked by the rows of houses on the two streets. He softened the corner until it amost disappeared completely, and the building therefore seems more round than rectangular. Thus, strictly speaking, the house arches across the two streets. Gaudí took up the idea of a rotunda, an oversized tower, in

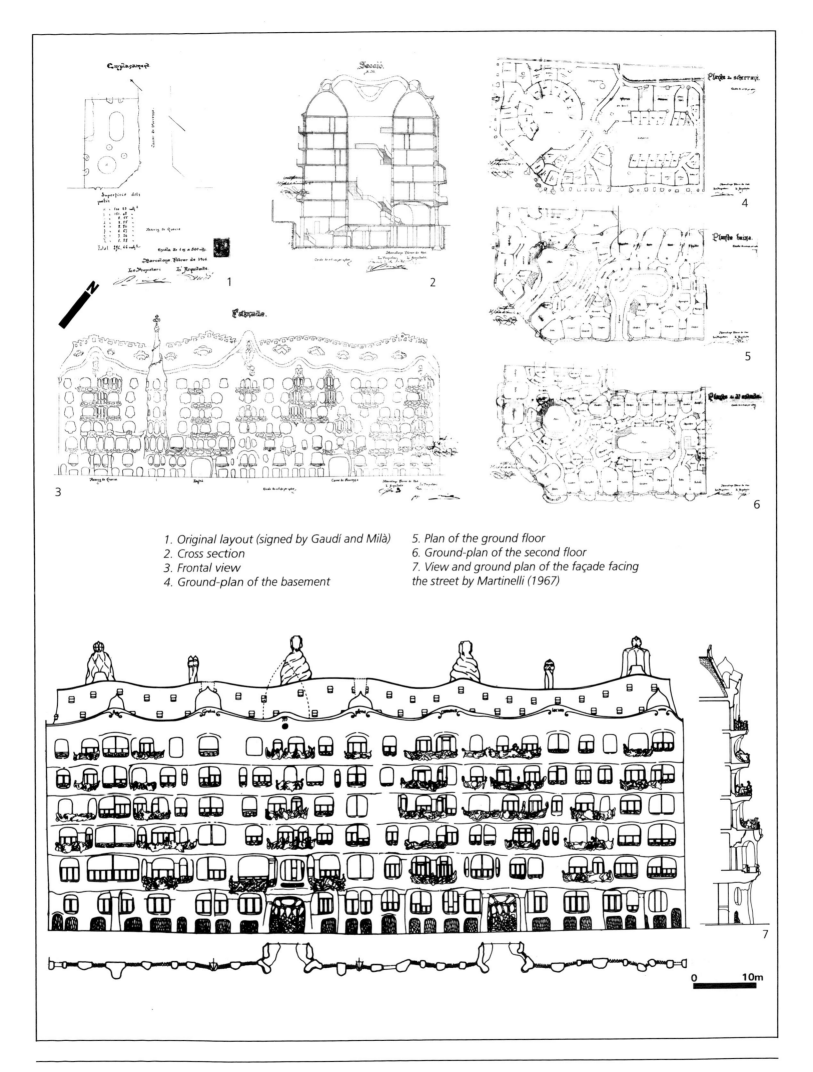

1. Original layout (signed by Gaudí and Milà)
2. Cross section
3. Frontal view
4. Ground-plan of the basement
5. Plan of the ground floor
6. Ground-plan of the second floor
7. View and ground plan of the façade facing the street by Martinelli (1967)

0   10m

designing two of the courtyards which had to be large to provide enough light in the building. Here, again, he was treading virgin territory. Almost every one of his projects involved some such innovation, which usually, although with some delay, found its way into Barcelona's architecture. In the Casa Milà, Gaudí replaced the usual square patios with round courtyards that grew outwards as they moved upwards. Aerial views of the building give the impression that these inner courtyards suck everything magically towards them, not just air and light: they are enormous funnels. The slanting walls at the end of these shafts enabled Gaudí, as if merely in passing, to provide excellent lighting even for the attic. All these ideas are not ornamental in nature but rather serve utterly practical goals. This is another difference between the Casa Milà and the Casa Batlló. The Casa Milà is important not least because one can perceive in it a synthesis of Gaudí's late stylistic elements. And it is almost a matter of course that this synthesis involved Gaudí in a number of tussles with the municipal building authorities.

As in the Casa Batlló, a column in the façade juts out over the pavement by a full 3 feet. There was no question of removing it. The city wanted to permit the columns, but only if the projecting part of them was dispensed with. In an apparently quite conciliatory mood, Gaudí agreed, although on the condition that he be allowed to erect a plaque at the site stating the reasons why the columns had been thus mutilated – upon which the city withdrew its objections. The second confrontation with the authorities occurred when Gaudí once again exceeded the maximum height permitted. This was entirely predictable because Gaudí made a habit of continually changing his buildings in the course of their construction. Here again Gaudí emerged victorious: the attic he had planned was installed.

Below: Iron gate of the entrance leading onto the Calle de Provença (left). The stairs leading up to the first floor from the courtyard (right).

Page 185: The rounded archways gleaming white in the light are the most striking design principle used in the attic rooms.

Page 186/187: The exit from the stairwell and Gaudí's bizarrely designed chimney pots on the roof.

Something that happened during construction work, however, caused Gaudí to lose interest in the building; he left it unfinished, although all that remained to be done was detailed finishing touches. Gaudí had planned to mount a series of dedications to the Virgin Mary on the façade. Indeed, he had designed a niche in which a haloed figure of Mary was to be placed holding the Infant Jesus in her arms, surrounded by two angels, one worshipping her, the other, armed with a sword, protecting the holy figures from enemies. During construction work there was a hefty, indeed even bloody uprising against the clergy in Barcelona. In the course of this "Semana Trágica" (from July 26 – 30, 1909), countless convents in the city went up in flames. In view of the anti-religious groundswell among the population, the owner of the building (and even his religious wife) judged it inappropriate to adorn the building with a series of religious representations and allusions – especially considering that it had already caused a stir. On this issue, Gaudí was not able to gain acceptance for his views, and the relationship between him and the owner was noticeably cooler thereafter.

Perhaps it was, after all, a good thing that Gaudí, who had become quite religious in the meantime and incorporated an increasing number of religious symbols in his buildings, did not integrate such elements in the Casa Milà as would have fitted better in the Sagrada Familia. In the absence of these sculptures, the outer façade of the building – as revolutionary as it may appear – seems to have been cast from one mould, though not with the "sugar icing" which is so typical of the Casa Batlló. Gaudí restricted himself to undressed stone to cover the outer walls – the surface seems to follow no clear plan. Continually changing waves, bulges and niches create the overall impression of something asymmetrical, something "natural". This impression prompted observers and critics to draw all sorts of comparisons, which, however, all miss their mark. The house was called *La Pedrera* colloquially, i.e. "the quarry." Yet, it is really only the colour and the surface that might be vaguely reminiscent of a quarry. Viewed from above, the house almost seems like the waves on the sea; yet, the line of waves is too smooth and harmonious for such an association. The Casa Milà is truly incomparable, and can be compared at most with Gaudí's own works. One might, for example, recollect the long writhing bench in Güell Park, or the line of waves that tops the Casa Milà's roof and which also takes up the lines of the floors below.

Nothing about this house is uniform. The ground-plans of each floor do not resemble one another. Gaudí was only able to create such a highly-varied spatial structure because, as was hinted at in earlier projects, he mostly dispensed with carrying walls. There is not one to be found in the whole Casa Milà complex. Everything is borne by numerous pillars and supports. The rooms are of differing heights in keeping with the wavy form of the façade.

The whole building is less a house and more an enormous sculpture that seems to have been moulded by hand from soft plasticine. Rather than comparing it with nature, one does more justice to the house if one refers to a series of formal associations, for Gaudí was, above all, fascinated by plastic forms. "The forms in this unusual house seem to have been thrust, stretched and forged outwards from the innermost centre of it and then welded into unity. The outside and the inside, the concave and the convex, the whole and the individual parts, the walls and the roof are all one

184

Chimney pots in a wide variety of forms. The characteristics of Gaudí's style can be seen most clearly here.

undivided whole, pulsating with the same rhythm. What is usually termed a façade becomes a wide, wavy space in vertical terms; it becomes an indented whole where otherwise a window would be. And in horizontal terms, what had until modern times been regarded as a roof becomes a moving landscape." (Josef Wiedemann)

The harmony and yet variety of the façade corresponds to the design of the interior. There are no straight lines inside: everything appears to have been modelled and seems plastic. In the bulges and rounded cavities there is a continuous alternation of light and darkness, as if the light was performing some kind of dance. In this house one continually comes across new surprises. Even strict reminiscences of the Colegio Teresiano in the attic apartments, which are supported by white arching walls, fit in perfect-

ly with the house. The roof sports a humorous landscape of almost surrealist sculptures that are in fact chimneys and air ducts. These are works of art that were only to be repeated at a later date in art history – but in sculpture, not in architecture, so that Gaudí's Casa Milà remained unique.

Above all, the house remained misunderstood for many years, and almost inevitably numerous parodies sprang up. But this also shows that, for all the ridicule that the building had to put up with, it nevertheless exercised a certain fascination over the public of its time – a fascination that was based unfortunately only on its external details. What was completely forgotten was that Gaudí's design for the Casa Milà was, as ever, based on practical considerations that were path-breaking; an example would be his forerunner of the underground garage in the basement.

Sagrada Familia

1883 – 1926

If piles of stones, scaffolding and huge cranes were
not part of the everyday furnishings of the church,
one would be tempted to go to the main portal
and enter this house of God. From the east, the
mighty building appears to be complete – a church
in the Gothic tradition and yet completely a typical
piece of 20th century architecture, and indeed one
that has taken a whole century to build. Gaudí
began to direct its construction over 100 years
ago, and today – decades after his death – the
outer walls exist only in rudimentary state. The
main portal will take quite a while still, and work
on its façade has not been started.
Should this church ever be finished, then it would
burst all dimensions asunder, and the first service
would ring out like the choirs of Heaven: there is
room for 1,500 singers, 700 children and 7 organs
on the choir galleries. But for the moment, such a
goal still seems to be a long way off.

Page 191: Overall view of the eastern façade. The apse is on the right-hand side.

It is probably impossible to find a church building anything like it in the entire history of art. One can normally speak of an artist's crowning achievement, often his last project, but in Gaudí's case one cannot. His main opus is at the same time his life's work. Gaudí was engaged on the Sagrada Familia throughout his life. Yet no one would have anticipated such a lengthy process, least of all Gaudí when, in 1883, at the age of 31, he began to direct the construction work. For a long time he seems to have been filled with optimistic hopes with respect to the project's completion. In 1886 he still believed that he would complete the Sagrada Familia in as little as ten years as long as he was given a sum of 360,000 pesetas per year. Financial support was by no means guaranteed, for the church had been planned as a church of atonement, and the intention was to fund it entirely on the basis of donations. This led to considerable delays in construction work during World War I: Gaudí went from house to house in person collecting funds.

The fact that in 1906 the church was still far from complete – work had got as far as the middle of one of the three (!) main façades – also had much to do with Gaudí's style of building. When he took on directing things he had a predominantly professional interest in the task. It was his first major construction project, he had been interested in church architecture for quite a while, but at the time he was fairly sceptical emotionally with regard to the Church. And scepticism was what he felt when studying the plans Villars had already drawn up. He could not and would not continue in the vein of the latter's Neo-Gothic approach. However, the digging of the crypt – over which the apse was then to be erected – had already been completed; the columns in the crypt had indeed already reached quite a height. Gaudí would of course have much preferred to give the building a completely new direction, but he was obliged to work with what had already been achieved. And Villars' columns far from pleased him. Yet, he held himself in check with regard to alterations. Admittedly, for a time he contemplated adding his own columns to those by Villars which were already there, but then realized that this would just lead to a nonsensical "civil war among the columns." The crypt as a consequence only bears Gaudí's trademarks to a limited extent. Nevertheless, he expanded Villars' porthole-like windows and moved the arches higher, so that the room received much more light and was not as oppressive as it had been in Villars' plan.

Gaudí's real achievements start with the apse over the crypt. Although the Gothic tradition remained as a valid source of inspiration, Gaudí cleansed it of all superfluous forms. While retaining the Gothic window, he loosened its formal stringency by counterbalancing different circular elements to it. Seven chapels fan out from the altar which is, by this very act, already in the visual centre of the building. What is more, the altar is free of all the overflowing ornamentation – typical for centuries – that tends to almost smother the altars of so many churches. This already demonstrates just how carefully Gaudí bore the religious functions of the church in mind. During his work on the Sagrada Familia he studied not only the ecclesiastical form of architecture, but also, and repeatedly, the liturgy of church services.

Page 194: The central part of the eastern façade. The four bell-towers are dedicated to the four saints Barnabas, Peter, Judae and Matthew. In the background, the towers from the façade of the Passion.

Page 195: Group of bell-towers on the eastern façade inscribed "Sanctus, Sanctus, Sanctus" ("Holy, holy, holy").

Yet the reason why the work was delayed so much was not only because Gaudí had to take over from another architect, but rather Gaudí's own

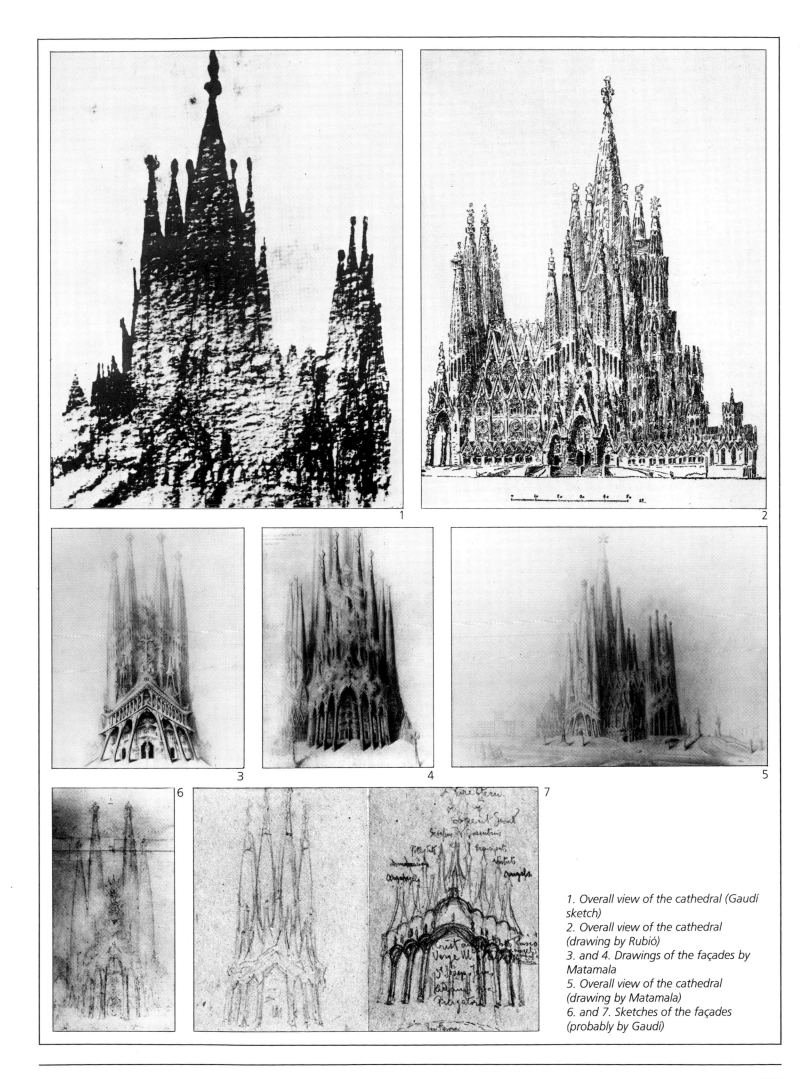

1. Overall view of the cathedral (Gaudí sketch)
2. Overall view of the cathedral (drawing by Rubió)
3. and 4. Drawings of the façades by Matamala
5. Overall view of the cathedral (drawing by Matamala)
6. and 7. Sketches of the façades (probably by Gaudí)

approach. Instead of following a pre-determined plan, he preferred to evolve the project during the actual construction work. No other building bears better testimony to this method than the Sagrada Familia. It is noteworthy that his first drawings for construction work say little about the construction itself. At most they convey a general impression of the building complex as planned, i.e. they are more or less atmospheric portraits.

An example of Gaudí's ever-changing mode of construction, following ever new insights, is the design or rather the development of the towers, the symbol of the church – if not landmark for Barcelona as a whole. The overall model envisaged twelve bell-towers, four for each of the three main façades. Gaudí started them as rectangular towers; they serve to frame the three respective portals that adorn each façade. It then emerged that the column-like towers would protrude quite sharply above the portals. Gaudí did not like this and therefore decided to make them round, with fascinating results.

Although the towers taper towards the top, they have nothing in common with the traditional sharply-pointed Gothic spires. Instead Gaudí resorted to a formal innovation he had already used successfully in the Colegio Teresiano. He designed the towers as rotational parabolas. The structure of the façade thus thrusts upward to quite a height. The sharply pointed portals create a similar impression as in Gothic cathedrals, although – like the apse windows – the sharpness of their appearance is softened by the incorporation of circular elements; and the rows of windows that lead up the towers as if in a spiral almost wrench the observer along with them. The upward thrust of the towers is, however, lessened by their rounded tops. Furthermore, Gaudí placed a crowning boss on each tower, ending all upward movement. Viewed from afar, these bosses have the appearance of enormous bishop's mitres. Indeed, Gaudí wanted to allude to the further history of Christianity – each tower is dedicated to one of the Apostles. Just as the Apostles turned into bishops, so too do the twelve towers each turn into a sort of mitre, and the whole tower seems to be an episcopal shepherd's crook.

This shows a typical feature of the Sagrada Familia. While the portals and towers initially seem to be designed purely in terms of architecture – full of imagination, but meaningful in terms of civil engineering – each of the church's different elements also has a second, symbolic function that was of even greater importance to Gaudí. There is nothing surprising about Bible scenes being used as "illustrations" on cathedrals. The Sagrada Familia has its share of them – indeed such a wealth can be encountered almost nowhere else. Gaudí did not just want to build a house of God, a place of worship, he conceived of the church as a catechism in stone, an oversized "book" in which the observer could read. This can be seen in the recurrent tendency to use symbols. The twelve towers, given their traditionality, are but a poor example. Yet they point to a central underlying structural characteristic. Gaudí imagined the church as the mystical Body of Christ. The centre is Christ himself, represented inside by the altar. Christ is, above all, the head of this body – as is symbolized by the cathedral's main spire, which is crowned with a great cross and alludes to Christ as the Saviour of mankind. The twelve towers that rise above the façades like crowns correspond to Christendom as a whole, represented by the Twelve Apostles.

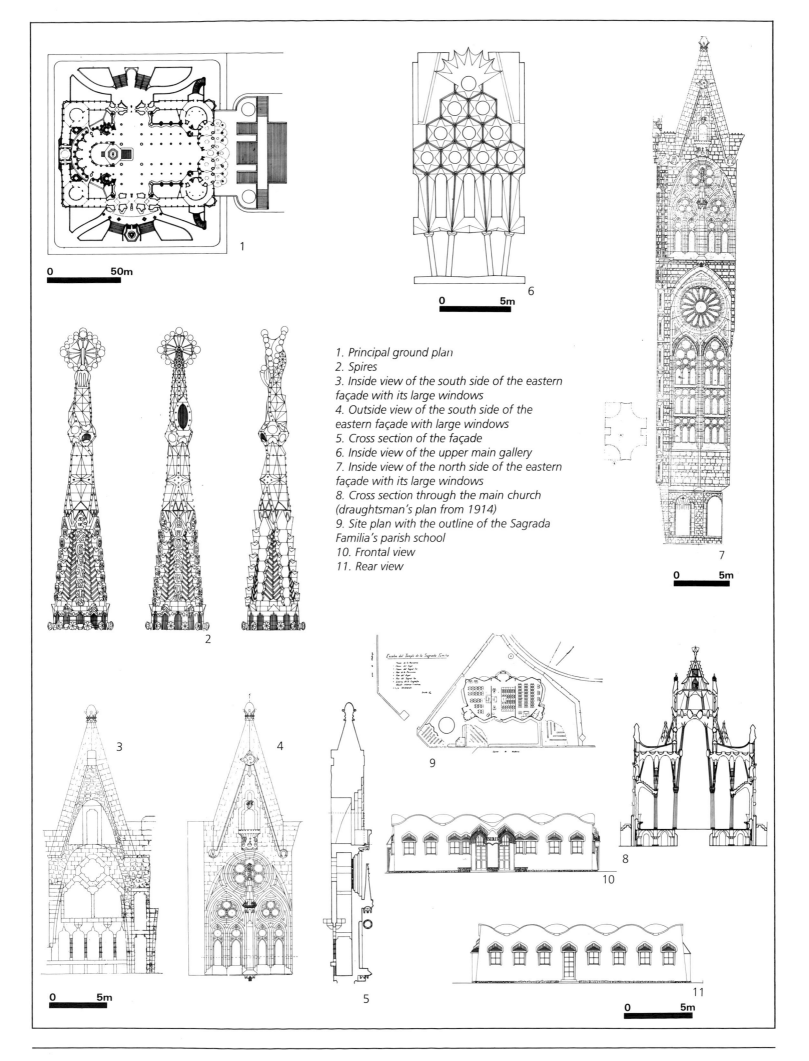

1. Principal ground plan
2. Spires
3. Inside view of the south side of the eastern façade with its large windows
4. Outside view of the south side of the eastern façade with large windows
5. Cross section of the façade
6. Inside view of the upper main gallery
7. Inside view of the north side of the eastern façade with its large windows
8. Cross section through the main church (draughtsman's plan from 1914)
9. Site plan with the outline of the Sagrada Familia's parish school
10. Frontal view
11. Rear view

0   50m

0   5m

0   5m

0   5m

0   5m

All of this clearly has to be supplemented by one's imagination. Gaudí himself was not even able to witness the final completion of the main apse. The eastern façade, with which he started the main building, also remained incomplete. At the time of Gaudí's death only three of the four eastern towers had been finished. Of the three façades planned, he himself almost completed only the eastern one. The rest exists merely as a plan and a plaster model (which, however, was destroyed by fire during the Spanish Civil War, and had to be reconstructed). Yet, it is precisely the design of the façades that bears the imprint of Gaudí's conception. Each of the façades is dedicated to one aspect of Christ's ministry. By means of realistic and symbolic presentation and allusions, Christ appears as a human on earth, as the Saviour of mankind and as the judge over life and death on the Day of Judgment. Gaudí himself, however, was only able to portray Christ's life on earth. And there are thematic reasons why he started work on the eastern façade, the "Christmas façade". Friends and advisors had wanted him to start work on the western façade first, which would have attracted the inhabitants' attention more than the eastern, which faced away from the city (at that time). The western wall was, however, devoted to the sufferings of Christ in Gaudí's plans. It was Gaudí's opinion that to start with it might have frightened people away. And he was probably right. In keeping with the somewhat sad, pessimistic theme of the façade, it lacks all ornamentational decoration, and is dominated by crass and ugly forms. In contrast, with reference to Christ's life, Gaudí was able to choose more

readily understandable forms of portrayal. Gaudí instilled the Flight to Egypt with hopes for the future. John the Baptist and his prophesy, and Jesus, showing the scribes what the true meaning of the words are – all this is portrayed simply and almost naïvely in numerous niches, almost as if presented as a Nativity play. This is reinforced by the names of the three portals. At the centre there is the Portal of Love, the largest of the three, depicting the birth of Christ and including a pelican as a symbol of love. It is flanked on the left by the Portal of Hope, which also portrays the two cruel events in Christ's childhood, namely Herod's murder of the children and the Flight to Egypt. Finally, there is the Portal of Faith to the right of the main gate – with corresponding scenes from the Bible such as the Revelation of St. John the Divine. There is a symbolic reason for these optimistic motives being carved into the eastern façade. "Ex oriente lux" – light comes from the East, and with it salvation, whereas the sufferings of Christ are depicted on the opposite western side, where the sun goes down. Light, which plays such an important role in Gaudí's secular buildings, is used here predominantly in a symbolic manner. This is true both of the compass direction of the main portal and of the use of lighting. The main tower as Gaudí planned it, soaring up above all else and symbolizing Christ, was to be lit up by spotlights from the twelve *"towers of the Apostles."* At the same time, it was Gaudí's intention to beam strong light from the cross – in which the tower was meant to end – over the city, to light up the people and thus to illustrate Christ's words: "I am the light."

Depiction of the Annunciation on the Portal of Love (left). Herod's murder of the children on the Portal of Hope (right).

Colours were also used symbolically. Gaudí intended, for example, to use green for the Portal of Hope. With its rather more joyful themes, the eastern façade as a whole was meant to be bright and colourful, whereas Gaudí wanted to have the façade of Suffering in somber colours. He certainly did not want to leave the stone in its natural hues. Gaudí hated monotony of colour – he found it unnatural. Nature, he frequently preached, never showed itself monochromatically or in complete uniformity of colour, for it always contained a more or less clear contrast of colours. For Gaudí, who in the course of his life felt increasingly influenced by Mother Nature as a teacher, this meant that the architect was called upon to give all the elements of architecture at least some touch of colour. This colour design, however, remained at least for the time being a pipe dream, as did the façade which was probably intended as the most important one, i.e. the southern façade. It was supposed to be a special witness to the Glory of God, and a wide staircase was to lead up to it. The themes were to be Death and Hell, the Fall from Grace, the hard work of everyday life that resulted from this and, finally, the Creed as a statement of faith and therefore the first step towards salvation.

The Creed, as so often in Gaudí's work, is depicted not in pictorial terms, but in the form of letters. It was to flare up between the bell towers in glowing letters. This method was used in the parts of the church that were completed last: on the eastern façade "Sanctus, Sanctus, Sanctus" can be read in the middle of the spiralling openings of the bell towers, directing one's eyes upwards – almost like a joyful cheer at the ascent into Heaven. Gaudí had always liked integrating letters, indeed even complete words, in his buildings, Güell Park showing the most instances. In the Sagrada Familia, the letters usually have a symbolic function, and they are intended to point repeatedly to the essential messages conveyed by the church building, which is more than the House of God: it is, in reality, a work of art shaped not unlike a sculpture. Often we do not know where one sculpture starts and the other finishes. Using a technique similar to that adopted in the Casa Milà, the façade of the Sagrada Familia is built mainly of material other than stone, and we get the impression that the sculpture consists of numerous ornaments moulded out of soft material – clay or wax – which then frame or cover the biblical scenes.

Page 202: Mary and Joseph worshipping Christ. Portrayal on the Portal of Love in the eastern façade.

Below: Sculpture of a snail (left). The base of a pillar next to the Portal of Love. It depicts a tortoise (right).

Page 205: Jesus can be seen as a carpenter in the foreground of this representation on the Gate of Faith.

Pages 206/207: Towers in the apse and the provisional altar. Work on the subterranean crypt has already been finished.

The letters lend emphasis to the messages conveyed by the scenes. One encounters anagrams, for example, of Jesus, Mary and Joseph in the windows of the apse. In contrast to most Biblical portrayals, Joseph is given a very predominant position here. This is understandable, given that the church was built at the instigation of the "Association of Worshippers of St. Joseph." The main chapel in the crypt is dedicated to him, and an effigy is to be found on the main portal of the eastern façade. The frequent depiction of a bee can be taken as a symbol of the industriousness of the worker. Yet there are even clearer signs of the status to which Joseph has been raised in this church. There are repeated portrayals of his tools. A large statue shows Jesus exercising his "foster-father's" profession — with a chisel in one hand. In Gaudí's presentation of the scene where Mary and Joseph search for their son, who is sitting with the scribes in the synagogue, it is Joseph who leads the way — unlike the usual depictions in which Mary leads the search. And, finally, Joseph is portrayed as guardian of the church: as the helmsman, he steers the ship (the church) safely past all dangers.

In the face of this wealth of symbolic allusions, which fuse the church — at least its façades — into a "picture" with expressive power, one might be tempted to forget Gaudí, the great master builder. The abundant ornamentation of the eastern façade slightly deceives us into overlooking the fact that, with the Sagrada Familia, Gaudí succeeded in creating an imposing piece of architecture. It shows his roots in tradition, although his personal style is forever in evidence. The ground-plan follows that of the main examples of Gothic cathedrals: the Sagrada Familia was conceived of as a basilica with five naves, and a transept with three aisles (the three portals in the eastern and western façades respectively are the entrances to the transept's three aisles). The ground-plan thus has the shape of a cross. The main nave, including the apse, was to be 311 feet long, the transept 196

Below: Depiction on the Portal of Hope of the Flight to Egypt, a work by Lorenzo Matamala (left). Sculpture next to the Portal of Love, showing domestic animals and plants from the Holy Land (right).

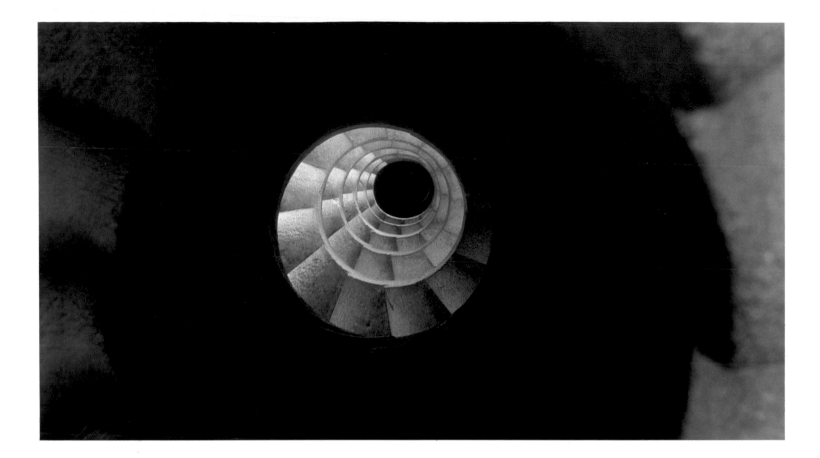

View from below of the spiral staircase in one of the towers. Room was left in the middle of the spiral for the installation of a cylindrically shaped bell.

feet. This corresponds largely with the shape of Cologne Cathedral (which Gaudí on the whole viewed positively). With such dimensions, however, it is obvious that there are problems of civil engineering. Cologne Cathedral has enormous columns and flying buttresses – the "crutches" Gaudí condemned Gothic architecture for having used. He manages without these aids. The Sagrada Familia is the best example of Gaudí's fundamental discovery that an interlinking of parabolic arches and slanting columns can bear the hefty weight of even large vaulting masonry. He had already proved this on a small scale in the Colegio Teresiano and the riding hall on the Güell Estate, in fact even in his first project, the factory halls of Mataró. In the Sagrada Familia he combined this construction principle with the insights he had gained from studying nature. With regard to load-bearing capacity, he took the eucalyptus tree as his example. It thus comes as no surprise that the network of columns in the main nave of the Sagrada Familia resembles a forest of stone. One gets the impression that the slanting columns cannot actually bear the weight from above; yet, Gaudí's buildings have always proved to be durable. The degree to which his successors bungled the work on the Bishop's Palace in Astorga shows just how precarious it can be to deviate from Gaudí's constructions, carefully rehearsed and tested beforehand by means of models.

His unique construction of columns has a surprising side effect. The aisles of the church appear etherially light. The columns seem to bear no weight. Gaudí said that in his work the Classical contrast in architecture between burdening and bearing was overcome in a positive sense. A column in the eastern façade illustrates this theory: Gaudí took as the base of the pillar two giant stone tortoises. The columns seem to grow up out of the carapaces, in other words to sprout upwards although they should really crush the animals. One seldom finds so graphic a realization of theory.

Gaudí's achievements as a building constructor also give cause for scepticism. There is hardly another architect who concerned himself so much with all the different tasks that arise on a building site. In fact, in the last years of his life, Gaudí lived in his small workshop on the site. He was to be encountered everywhere, devoting attention to the smallest of engineering problems. And he was just as clear about how to solve them as he was on the large-scale constructional problems. He left behind him models that showed how he conceived the finished church to look, but it is questionable whether it can ever be completed without him.

Even César Martinell, a friend of Gaudí's, had a sceptical, if humorous, opinion of the problem. He stated that the church should be regarded as completed and that this was more than just an optimistic approach considering that Gaudí had not finished a single façade. In fact, he maintained their completion was still a very long way off.

He was not exaggerating. Indeed, the continuation of Gaudí's projects after his death would seem to prove the point. The eastern façade is admittedly now complete, but it is still far too early to speak of the building as a church. The western façade has meanwhile started to take shape – and Gaudí's plans and models have been followed carefully. But work on it has taken up the last three decades: again and again one hears of yet another small portion being inaugurated. This might lead us to question whether work on the church should be continued at all. There were critics of the church even in Gaudí's day, but, with his vision of the building ever before his eyes, he was able to prevail in person. Nowadays, this persistence has to exist without Gaudí's dynamism to push it ahead. Not only the immense costs would speak against continuing construction efforts (by 1914, the project had already run into more than three million pesetas and Gaudí was still in the middle of it), but also the fact that there are plenty of uncom-

Pages 210/211: The inner side of the eastern façade. (page 210). The upper part of the towers in the eastern façade with the inscription "Hosanna in Excelsis" ("Hosanna in the highest") (page 211, above left). The inner side of the eastern façade (page 211, upper left). View from above on the eastern façade (page 211, below).

Vertiginous view from above looking down the spiral staircase in one of the towers.

The design of the spires are an example of Gaudí's imaginative creation of forms.

pleted Gaudí buildings. Indeed, it is almost a trademark of his that he did not finish his buildings. Yet, this must be balanced against Gaudí's statement that the Sagrada Familia was the first in a series of utterly new cathedrals. And that places an obligation on us – as does the fact that the Sagrada Familia has long since become the landmark of Barcelona. Even at a time when the first bell towers were still in their infancy, gradually taking on shape and stature, the inhabitants of the city already identified with "their" church. After all, the bell towers soar above the city (the two middle towers are both over 300 feet high; the main tower was planned to reach 557 feet). And finally, with this project Gaudí had rooted himself firmly in the grand tradition of mediaeval cathedral building. These were also not the work of one architect – but of whole generations. Gaudí has truly left his city a magnificent legacy, even if it is not without its problems.

This torso-like state of the church does have one advantage, however. Another miniature delicacy of Gaudí's has thus remained intact. The church was conceived as constituting the centre of a small "suburb":

workshops and in particular schools were to surround it. A parish school was erected. In Gaudí's plans it was to be torn down as soon as the ground was needed for the main church; the fact that the school is still standing attests to the state of the project. The school has an unpretentious appearance; and yet it is not without its charms. It is an illustration above all of Gaudí's practically-minded approach. The façade and roof remind one somewhat of the Casa Milà. The school building also has organically undulating surfaces. However, alongside its aesthetic charm, it also has practical advantages. Gaudí built it with the simplest of materials, i.e. bricks, which he so much preferred. The winding wavy structure of the façade gives it strength, just as the roof, moving in sine-shaped curves, has a certain stability: Le Corbusier was so taken by this construction that he immediately made a sketch of it. Two inside walls, that need not serve as carrying walls, divide the building into school rooms, whereby the siting of the walls can be altered without much difficulty as required. Functionality makes a small masterpiece out of this inconspicuous building.

This upper part of the Portal of Love depicts a cypress. The tree is a symbol of immortality owing to its durable wood and its ever-green branches (left). Spire on the eastern façade (right).

Pages 214/215: The school building attached to the Sagrada Familia.

Further Projects

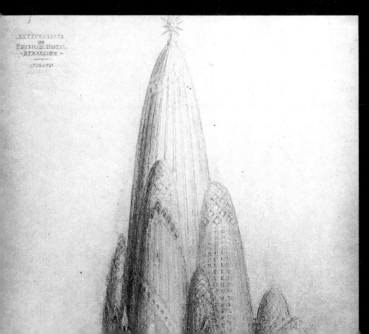

Below: Entrance gate to the Finca Miralles on the Passeig de Manuel Girona.

The Finca Miralles

While working on his first large apartment block — the Casa Calvet — Gaudí also took on a number of smaller jobs of secondary importance. Only the entrance gate that he built for the planned house of his friend, the factory-owner Hermengild Miralles, is of interest, not least because it is in strange contrast to the somewhat strict conception of Casa Calvet. In many ways this gateway already points forward to the world of forms Gaudí was to develop in his last secular buildings, the Casa Batlló, and above all the Casa Milà.

Anyone who faces this odd formation — there is hardly any other word to describe it — will spontaneously ask oneself how it can actually hold itself in place. It rises in a variety of suggested twists and turns from the ground like

some bizarre seashell. The outer contours follow the form of the actual archway, yet on the right-hand side they start a writhing life of their own. In the process, what seems to be a pillar is formed – and it appears that a coat of arms was to be inserted. Next to it, a door with iron bars seems to have been planned. The formation could have been invented a few decades later by Salvador Dali. "Preemptions" of Surrealism of this sort are not unusual in Gaudí's work. However, as if wishing to conceal his imagination of different shapes, he constructed a cornered roof of undressed stone that juts out over the seashell entrance. The supports for the roof are clearly visible – a characteristic hardly in evidence elsewhere in Gaudí's works, just as this triangular projecting sun roof-cum-shade is an exception. One could imagine this as the entrance gate to the Casa Milà; indeed, Gaudí was already anticipating his own work. The gateway was originally set into a perimeter wall. Today, it stands in the middle of a modern housing estate that will continue to expand. As a consequence, the gateway will soon be removed and rehoused in Güell Park.

The wall at the entrance to the Finca Miralles. The design of the wall covering resembles the writhing movements of a sea-serpent.

Bishop Campins i Barceló, who commissioned the restoration of the cathedral.

Palma Cathedral

Bishop Campins i Barceló first, who was still quite young at the time, first met Gaudí in 1899, on the building site of the Sagrada Familia. He talked with the architect for three whole hours and what fascinated him most was not so much Gaudí's purely architectonic abilities, but his vast knowledge of Church liturgy, the result of long discussions at the Bishop of Astorga's table. Campins had far-reaching plans: he wanted to redesign the interior of his church, or rather free it of some changes that had slowly occurred over the centuries, in other words give the church back some of its original character. When viewing several Gothic churches some years after his first visit to Barcelona he met Gaudí again and confided his plans to the architect, plans that had already been approved by the cathedral's chapter.

Gaudí must have been immediately fascinated by the project. After all, it posed a great challenge. It involved, above all, restructuring the whole middle nave. The choir stalls were in the centre of the church – in the middle nave – quite out of keeping with usual Gothic architecture, although Palma Cathedral was a masterpiece in the Catalonian Gothic style. No one was better acquainted with the task than Gaudí. Admittedly, though, he had not had a very favourable encounter with the chapter of Astorga Cathedral – an experience that was to be repeated in Palma. In 1902 Gaudí travelled to Palma to study the site and immediately drew up a whole series of plans. These centred on moving the choir stalls from the middle nave to the presbytery, close to the altar. This was in keeping with existing historical evidence and yet posed no small problem, although something similar had been carried out as early as the end of the 18th century in the Church of Santa Maria del Mar in Barcelona. Gaudí thus had examples which could serve as guidelines. Nevertheless, his achievements consisted not just in clearing the middle nave – which was subsequently at the sole disposal of the worshippers. The whole composition of the interior changed abruptly with this shift of a substantial and striking element of the previous building.

Gaudí expanded the forward part of the presbytery and also tried to increase the impression of space by covering the rear wall of the apse with bright metallic ceramic tiles. He did this in keeping with his own conception of natural polychromy, and came up against the protest of the Cathedral's chapter. Only Bishop Campins supported him. It was as if the Astorga experience was being repeated down to the last detail. The Cathedral's chapter had restoration in mind, the "re-creation" of the old – Gaudí, on the other hand, was interested in a "reformation" of the cathedral itself. He removed the 18th century Baroque altar and thus uncovered – quite in accordance with the chapter – the old Gothic altar, which had been consecrated in 1346.

By freeing the main nave of the choir stalls, Gaudí heightened the effect of spaciousness inside the building. And by means of some lights and several canopies he changed the historical face of the cathedral. His redesigning of the space around the altar exhibits the greatest excellence. A large, seven-cornered canopy was to replace the previous one, which was square and simple. Gaudí planned a complex interplay of symbolic references: the seven corners represented the Seven Gifts of the Holy Spirit; fifty lamps (seven times seven plus one) were to remind people of Pentecost. In addition, sculptures of Christ on the Cross, the Virgin Mary and St. John were included to refer to the act of Salvation. Gaudí also drew up plans for a magnificent illumination of the interior, using electrical lighting and panes of coloured glass. Only one side of the canopy is outfitted in this manner.

There may have been plans to continue with this work, but the difficulties with the cathedral's chapter increased. Gaudí's reform of the church building in terms of its ecclesiastical tasks went too far in the eyes of the priests – Gaudí was too creative. Had he completed his work, he would have imposed his style unmistakably on the building – and this would certainly not have been to the building's disadvantage. As it was, one can feel no more than a hint of his artistry – although he had numerous three-dimensional designs, using sculptures, in mind; one can see clear signs of the work on the Sagrada Familia.

In 1914, Gaudí abandoned work on the cathedral. Perhaps the experiences he had had in Palma played a role in his decision to take on no further contract work and to devote all his energy to the Sagrada Familia. While working on Palma Cathedral he obviously noticed, in his effort to attain perfection, that he was constantly in danger of turning something that seemed quite manageable at first into a series of tasks that could never be completed.

Canopy over the high altar in Palma Cathedral, as restored by Gaudí.

The Bishop's Palace in Astorga

If there is a building of Gaudí's to which the term Neo-Gothic applies, then it must surely be the Bishop's Palace in Astorga near León. The old palace had been destroyed by fire and in 1887 Bishop Juan Bautista Grau i Vallespinós commissioned Gaudí to design a new palace. Grau, like Gaudí, came from Reus. Before being ordained bishop, he had been the Vicar-General for the Archdiocese of Tarragona. The contract was not exactly timely as far as Gaudí was concerned; he was in the middle of drawing up plans for the Sagrada Familia, and work on the Güell Palace was still under way. Gaudí did not make a simple project of the task. He requested that he be given exact plans of the site and photographs of the surroundings: it was above all the latter that played an important part in his design of the exterior of the building. The bishop was delighted with the plans; the San Fernando Academy in Barcelona, whose approval was necessary before work could go ahead, was somewhat more reserved. This was just a foretaste of the problematic situation Gaudí was to experience during

The main façade of the Bishop's Palace in Astorga. The zinc angels flanking the approach to the entrance were originally intended to be mounted on the roof.

1. Ground-plan of the first floor (the main floor)
2. Ground-plan of the attic floor
3. Frontal view from the south east.
4. Vertical section

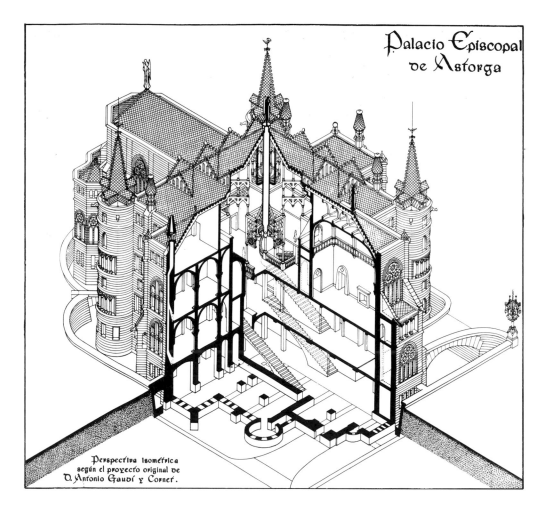

Perspectiva isométrica según el proyecto original de D. Antonio Gaudí y Cornet.

True-to-scale three-dimensional drawing following a draft by Gaudí.

construction work until building activities were broken off prematurely in 1893. As long as his patron, the bishop, was still alive, Gaudí managed to put his ideas into practice, after he had twice revised plans to suit the wishes of the Academy. Quite out of keeping with his later custom, Gaudí drafted precisely drawn plans for the building, apparently in part because he wanted to preempt the objections he anticipated.

Gaudí oriented himself above all towards the Neo-Gothicism propagated by Viollet-le-Duc, which was in line with the character and function of the building. This theorist had recommended that an intensive study of old Gothic buildings should precede any new architecture, but had advised strictly against simply copying such forms.

Gaudí perfected this undertaking. He approximated his work so closely to his historical models that he even used French Gothic capitals for the columns on the main floor: the eight-pronged, star-shaped abacuses are direct imitations of the Sainte Chapelle in Paris. The sense of Gothicism surrounding the building is otherwise not pronounced. The round towers remind one more of a castle than a sacred building. Although the starkly protruding entrance contains monumental arches, they have been flattened out so that they do not thrust upwards but seem rather more to bow forward. The apexes of the windows are also only mildly pointed. It is only the dining room on the first floor that has predominantly Gothic traits. Nevertheless, some critics have described this building as the best example of Spanish Neo-Gothic architecture.

Gaudí used white granite for the outer façade. This material was adopted because of the fascination it exerted on the eye, but it also had a spiritual function for Gaudí: the bishop's palace was supposed to accord optically with the white of the bishop's robes. This white façade was to climax gloriously in the equally white roof, but things never got that far. Bishop Grau died before building work was completed, and from the very beginning the administration of the diocese had not held Gaudí's plans in particularly high esteem. Following the bishop's death, it tried to intervene in the work, whereupon Gaudí abandoned the project. It is said that he even intended to burn the plans, which he then did not do. It was his wish that the building remain unfinished; he swore himself never to set foot in Astorga again, not even to cross over it in a balloon.

It was some time before the building was completed. The architects who took up the work deviated from his plans so that part of the building collapsed. It was not ready for habitation until 1961.

The dining-room on the first floor of the Bishop's Palace in Astorga.

The Casa de los Botines

As Gaudí had meanwhile established contacts with a wealth of people, the number of works he was contracted to do increased. While still undertaking the last work on the Bishop's Palace in Astorga (difficulties were already looming on the horizon with the administration of the diocese) he was commissioned to construct a further building in León. Two Gaudí buildings in such a small town – what opulence! At the end of the 19th century León had a mere 16,000 inhabitants and was not exactly distinguished by architectonic highlights. A few larger buildings from the past at least gave the face of the town some substance: a cathedral built between the 13th and 15th centuries, the large monastery of St. Marcos and a somewhat sober Renaissance palace.

Gaudí's work was not carried out under a particularly lucky star. His design for the foundations was not in keeping with the usual style of building in the town; people bemoaned the absence of pillars, and when Gaudí constructed the bases for the turrets on the first floor, turrets which he had intended as decoration for the sides of the building, there was a general fear that the Casa de los Botines (named after the father of the financial sponsor of the project, Joan Homs i Botinàs) would topple over. The building stood firm despite all the forebodings and today still shows no signs of age: it has meanwhile become the seat of the local savings bank.

Gaudí was not completely free of blame for the frosty attitude of the inhabitants; he had never mixed with the people and had only conversed with the bishop. Indeed, he had by then given up his opposition towards the clergy; the long talks with the Bishop of Astorga had not been without their influence on him. His dandy-like external appearance had given way to a rather more ascetic look and he had had his beard and long hair cut.

The people who commissioned Gaudí to build the Casa de los Botines, the Fernández brothers (after whom this building is sometimes referred to as the Casa Fernández), were primarily interested in a building for commercial purposes that would house a few apartments for rent in the upper storeys. Gaudí kept strictly to these functional aspects in his plans: storage rooms in the basement, office rooms above. The first few floors needed no carrying walls, an anticipation of Gaudí's later work. If we disregard a few

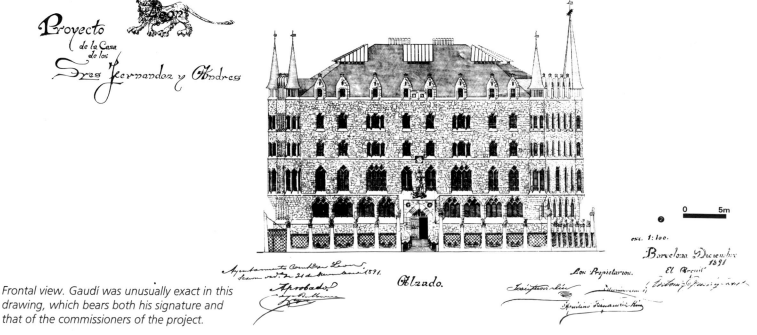

Frontal view. Gaudí was unusually exact in this drawing, which bears both his signature and that of the commissioners of the project.

ornamental components, then Gaudí constructed a somewhat Spartan building. It stands on the central square in Léon, the Plaza de San Marcelo, like some large mass of stone. In contrast to the hefty underlying form, Gaudí – in keeping with his style at the time – made use of Neo-Gothic elements, but only sparingly. The windows are often divided into three parts, which makes them seem broad, and are rounded at the top. Only the oriels that rise out of the edge of the roof have a spiky Gothic shape. The building clearly belongs in the trio of Gaudí's buildings inspired by Gothic architecture, and, together with the Bishop's Palace in Astorga and the Colegio Teresiano, can be viewed as constituting a distinctive series in Gaudí's opus. Today, it still towers above the rest of the town, and the inhabitants have obviously grown accustomed to it. Gaudí mounted a statue of St. George the Dragon-slayer above the main entrance. Plans in 1950 to remove this statue met with a general wave of protest. The sculpture stayed where it was. Nowadays, one does not go about disfiguring works of the famous Catalonian architect without thinking twice.

The main façade of the Casa de los Botines, which seems quite Spartan compared with Gaudí's other much more lavishly decorated houses.

Plans for a Hotel in New York

Gaudí had almost completed the Casa Milà when he was offered a second project that inevitably fascinated him, partly because of the sheer dimensions involved. In 1908, an American businessman was so taken with Gaudí's architecture that he asked him to build an enormous hotel in New York. Work never got further than a few drawings in the typical style in which Gaudí sketched his buildings at the time – yet these reveal much of what Gaudí was thinking as he turned his attention ever more closely to designing the Sagrada Familia. In formal terms, the Sagrada Familia was clearly the hotel's immediate predecessor. Had the project been realized, New York would have received a hotel that looked like a temple. Gaudí planned a building approximately 900 feet in height (more than twice that of the main tower planned for the Sagrada Familia). Based on a circular ground-plan, a central, parabolic tower, as in his other buildings, was to rise up like a huge spindle flanked by other high and steeply slanting rotundas – a grand embodiment of the gigantic proportions latent in the American dream of economic progress.

Right and page 229: Construction drawings for the New York hotel building.

Below: In 1892, Gaudí designed a building for the Catholic Mission in Tangiers. As in the case of the planned hotel in New York, the towers in this design anticipated the bell towers of Sagrada Familia.

The Güell Bodegas are on a hill with a superb view of the Mediterranean. The building was for many years attributed to Gaudí's friend, the architect Francesc Berenguer i Mestres. Most probably Gaudí and Berenguer collaborated on the project.

The Güell Bodegas

The *bodegas* (wine cellars) which Gaudí built for his patron Eusebi Güell in Garraf near Sitges are usually not mentioned in the literature on him, because for a long time they were attributed to the architect Francesc Berenguer i Mestres. Indeed, at first sight the building does not seem to be a typical Gaudí creation. Although the combination of undressed stone and brick passages bears some resemblance to Gaudí's buildings of the 1880s and 1890s, this stone combination was no invention of Gaudí's. He simply used it to decorate buildings, thus doubling up the pure construction material used as the ornamentation of the houses. The *bodegas* consist of a series of highly different architectonic forms. Above the storage cellars proper there is a floor with living quarters which is, in turn, underneath a chapel. In formal terms, this building is totally out of keeping with Gaudí's other works; even the very imaginative buildings of his early phase, inspired by Moorish architecture, bear no resemblance to it. And yet there are Gaudían structures everywhere: for example, the frequent use of parabolic arches — in the form of highly modern window arches, the entrance gate and a bridge that leads up to a mediaeval tower.

The roof also bears Gaudí's trademark — again not in terms of outward appearance, but in its very structure. "Sun shade and hat in one" is what Gaudí said he wanted his roofs to be, a principle put into perfect practice in the Casa Batlló. In the *bodegas* he went one step further. He planned the whole building with the arch-like shape of the roof as his starting-point. On one side it almost reaches the ground. The building is thus given the character of a tent, and has been compared with Far Eastern pagodas.

The porter's lodge contains a further characteristic feature of Gaudí's work. The archway over the entrance is closed by a gate of iron chains, which, although not as large as the Dragon Gate of the Güell estate, is nevertheless of considerable size. Just like the Dragon Gate, it is only hinged on one side, which makes it higher than the other. The basic shape of the gate is also the same as its dragon-like counterpart.

The pavilion at the entrance to the Güell Bodegas. The porter's lodge and the gate form one single unit.

Antoni Gaudí 1852 – 1926
His Life and Work

1852 Gaudí is born on the 25th of June in Reus, near Tarragona. His parents are Francesc Gaudí i Serra and Antònia Cornet i Bertran.

1863 – 1868 Gaudí attends secondary school in the Colegio de los Padres Escolapios, a monastic school in Reus.

1867 Gaudí publishes his first

Antoni Gaudí's parents' house in Riudoms (Tarragona).

drawings in the *El Arlequin* newspaper, distributed in handwritten copies in Reus (in an edition of twelve copies). Gaudí draws backdrops for school plays.

1869 – 1874 Gaudí attends preparatory courses in order to be eligible to study architecture at the Faculty of Natural Science at Barcelona University.

1870 He designs the coat of arms for the Abbot of Poblet Monastery during restoration work on the building.

1873 – 1877 Gaudí studies architecture at the Escola Provincial d'Arquitectura in Barcelona. During his studies he makes numerous drafts, among others the design for a cemetery gate, a central hospital for Barcelona and a landing stage for ships.
During his time at university, Gaudí spends his time working in architectural studios in order to earn money

– for example, under Josep Fontseré and Francisco de Paula de Villar, who is later to start the Sagrada Familia project. Gaudí and Villar work together with others on the building of the Montserrat monastery.

1876 Gaudí's mother dies.

1878 Shortly before finishing his studies, Gaudí is awarded his first public contract. He is commissioned to design street lights for the city of Barcelona, the first of which are installed in 1879.

Gaudí received his training at the Academy for Fine Arts.

On 15th March Gaudí receives his architect's diploma.

Gaudí designs the windows for Esteve Comella, a glove merchant. Eusebi Güell is so taken with the window that he first becomes aware of Gaudí's work.

At the same time, Gaudí works intensively on a project for the workers' cooperative settlement in Mataró. The project is on display at the World Exhibition in Barcelona. After completing his studies, Gaudí goes on trips with the Associación de Arquitectos de Cataluña and the Associación Catalanista d'Excursions Cientifíques in the vicinity of Barcelona in order to study old buildings.

Gaudí is commissioned by Manuel Vicens i Montaner to design an apartment building.

1879 Gaudí's sister, Rosita Gaudí de Egea, dies.

1881 Gaudí publishes an article on a craft exhibition in the daily paper, *La Renaixença.* It is Gaudí's only piece of journalism.

The plans had meanwhile taken shape for the Mataró workers' settlement. They were printed by the Jepús bookprinter's and were signed by Gaudí.

1882 Gaudí works closely with the architect Joan Martorell and, through the latter's agency, comes into close contact with Neo-Gothic architecture.

1883 He takes on a project designing a hunting pavilion for Eusebi Güell in Garraf (near Sitges).

On 3 November, Gaudí, at Martorell's suggestion, succeeds Villar on the Sagrada Familia project.

1883 – 1888 Gaudí works on the Casa Vicens, starts designing *El Capricho,* a country house in Comillas (near Santander) for Don Máximo Diaz de Quijano. As Gaudí continues to spend most of his time in Barcelona, he delegates supervision of the building work to the architect Cristófol Cascante i Colom.

1884 – 1887 Gaudí builds the entrance way and the stables for the Güell Estate in Les Corts. This is his first major work for Güell.

1886 – 1889 Gaudí builds a town palace for Güell in Barcelona. During work on this project he travels, accompanied by the second Margrave of Comillas, through Andalusia and Morocco – a sign of his growing fame.

1887 – 1893 Gaudí builds the Bishop's Palace in Astorga.

1888 – 1889 Gaudí works on the Colegio Teresiano.

1891 – 1892 The Casa de los Botines is built in León. At the same time, Gaudí travels to Málaga and Tangier in order to study the site for the planned Franciscan Mission that he is supposed to design.

1893 The Bishop of Astorga dies. Gaudí designs a hearse for his patron's funeral and the ledger for the

A view inside Gaudí's workshop at the Sagrada Familia. Note the numerous plaster casts.

Photo from Gaudí's identification card for the World Exhibition in Barcelona, in 1888.

grave; he abandons work on the Bishop's Palace owing to increasing disagreement between himself and the episcopal authorities.

1894 Gaudí fasts too stringently during Lent, showing how strongly religious he has by now become, whereas in earlier days he used to be somewhat cool toward religion.

1895 – 1901 Gaudí, together with his friend Francesc Berenguer i Mestres, constructs a set of wine cellars for Güell in Garraf (near Sitges). For many years, Gaudí's hand in the project remained unknown.

1898 Gaudí starts work on the plans of the church in the Güell Colony. Although the project drags on until 1916, it leaves a highly incomplete building behind: Gaudí built only the crypt and the entrance portal of the planned church.

1898 – 1900 Gaudí builds the Casa Calvet in Barcelona. In 1900,

the city awards him the prize for the best building of the year. This is the only public award Gaudí ever receives.

1900 Gaudí is commissioned to design the first Glorious Secret of the Rosary for a large Rosicrucian project in the Montserrat Monastery.

1900 – 1909 On the grounds of the former country house of Martí, Gaudí builds a country house for Maria Sagués in the style of a mediaeval castle. The building is on a slope above Barcelona and received its name "Bellesguard" from the good view it afforded.

1900 – 1914 In 1900, Gaudí commences work on Güell's most ambitious project, namely, to build a large park and housing settlement in Gràcia (at the time on the outskirts of Barcelona). Only two of the houses planned were actually built, at the entrance to the grounds. Up until 1914 Gaudí spends time designing the entrance way, the large terrace or square and the complex network of paths and roads.

The funeral procession in front of the Sagrada Familia, where Gaudí was buried.

1901 Gaudí constructs a perimeter wall and entrance gate for Miralles, a factory owner.

1903 – 1914 Gaudí restores Palma Cathedral in Mallorca, and attempts to recreate the old liturgical meaning which was originally given to the interior of the cathedral.

1904 – 1906 Gaudí undertakes alterations to the apartment block owned by Josep Batlló in Barcelona. The result is an adventurous style, revolutionary for the age.

1906 Gaudí moves into one of the houses in Güell Park in order to save his father having to climb stairs. His father dies on 29 October of the same year.

1906 – 1910 The Casa Milà is built – Gaudí's largest apartment house project.

1908 Gaudí is commissioned to build a hotel in New York. Things get only as far as draft design drawings, which reveal a daring constructional vision.
In the same year, Gaudí plans to erect a chapel for the Colegio Teresiano. The project is dashed by disagreement between Gaudí and the Mother Superior of the convent. Work is started on building the Güell Colony Crypt in Santa Coloma.

1909 Gaudí builds the Sagrada Familia parish school.

1910 Numerous works of Gaudí's are shown at the Société Nationale de Beaux-Arts Exhibition in Paris. This is the only exhibition of Gaudí's work outside Spain to be held in his lifetime.
Eusebi Güell is made a count.

1912 Gaudí's niece, Rosa Egea i Gaudí, dies at the age of 36.

1914 Gaudí's close friend and colleague, Francesc Berenguer i Mestres dies; Gaudí had received his first schooling in Reus together with Francesc from the latter's father. Gaudí decides to devote all his attention to the Sagrada Familia.

1926 On 7 June Gaudí is hit by a tram whilst out walking. He dies three days later in the Hospital de la Santa Creu in Barcelona.

Gaudí (on the left) explains the Sagrada Familia to Eusebi Güell and Bishop Torras i Bages.

The History of the Sagrada Familia

1866 Josep Bocabella i Verdaguer founds the Association of Worshippers of St. Joseph.

1875 The plan for a cathedral built after the Basilica in Loreto in Italy takes shape.

1877 The architect of the diocese, Francisco de Paula de Villar offers to draw a plan free of charge.

1882 On 19 March the first groundstone is laid in accordance with Villar's plan.

1883 On 3 November Gaudí starts work as architect of the Sagrada Familia after Villar had given notice.

1884 – 1887 The crypt is built.

1885 The Chapel of St. Joseph is consecrated. The eastern façade is built between 1891 and 1900.

1898 Gaudí decides to change the ground-plan of the bell towers on the eastern side. The original square outline is continued as a circular form.

1900 The ornamentative shell of the three portals in the eastern façade is completed. The bell towers have reached a height of 105 feet.

1906 From now on construction work moves sluggishly, owing to a lack of funding.

1914 In the absence of money, work comes to a complete standstill. Costs until now have amounted to 3.3 million pesetas. A plaster model of the whole church is made.

1918 Gaudí's final design for the Façade of the Passion (the western side) is completed.

1925 On 30 November the bell tower dedicated to St. Barnabas is consecrated.

1926 On 10 June Gaudí dies and is buried in the crypt.

1927 – 1930 Work on the final three bell towers on the eastern façade is concluded.

1936 Fire in the crypt. Gaudí's archives with the drawings and models is partially destroyed.

1954 The foundation walls for the western façade are laid.

1976 The 50th anniversary of Gaudí's death. The spires on the western façade are completed.

1985 The western façade itself is finished.

**Map showing the location
of Gaudí's works**

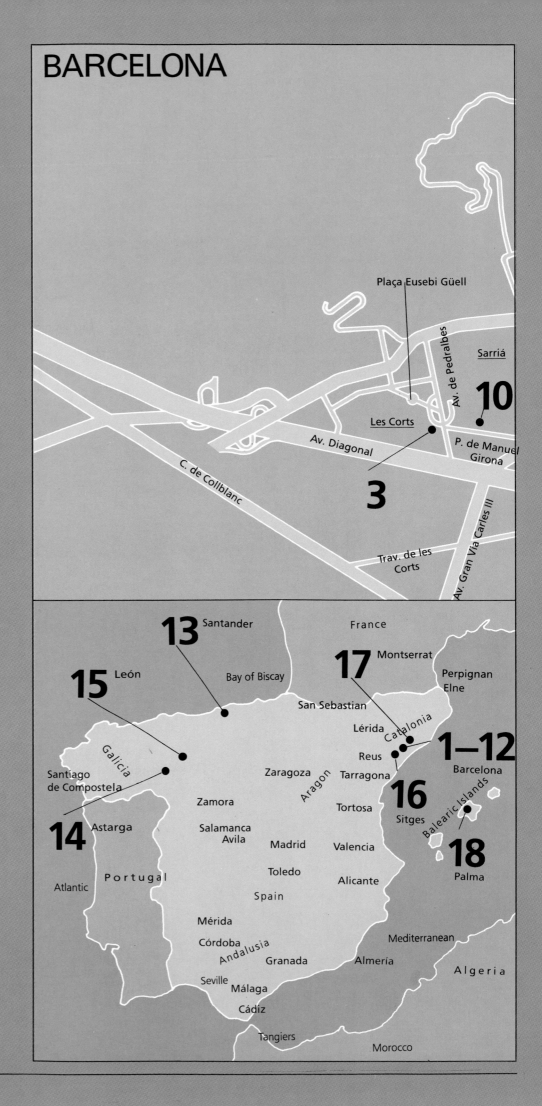

BARCELONA

Plaça Eusebi Güell

Sarriá

Av. de Pedralbes

10

Les Corts

Av. Diagonal

P. de Manuel
Girona

C. de Collblanc

3

Av. Gran Vía Carles III

Trav. de les
Corts

13 Santander

France

15 León

17 Montserrat

Bay of Biscay

Perpignan
Elne

San Sebastian

Lérida

Catalonia

1–12

Galicia

Reus

Barcelona

Santiago
de Compostela

Zaragoza

Aragon

Tarragona

Balearic Islands

Zamora

Tortosa

16

Salamanca
Avila

Madrid

Valencia

Sitges

18

14 Astarga

Toledo

Alicante

Palma

Atlantic

Portugal

Spain

Mérida

Córdoba

Andalusia

Granada

Almería

Mediterranean

Algeria

Seville

Málaga

Cádiz

Tangiers

Morocco

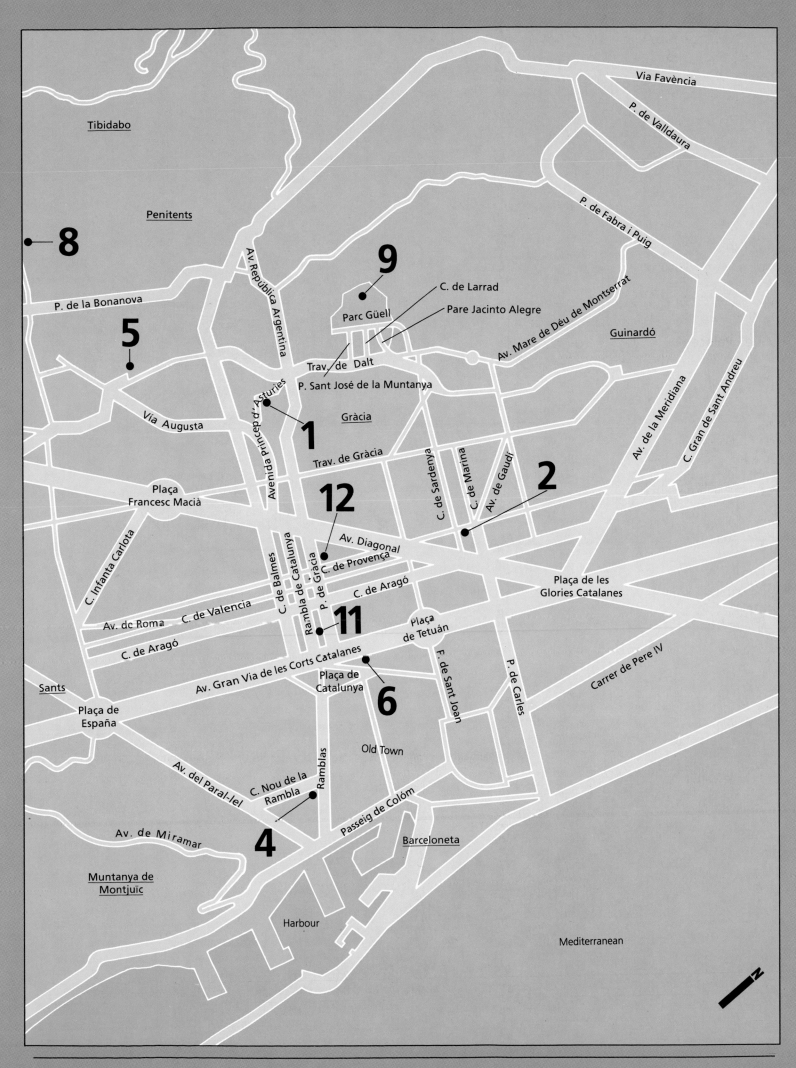

8

9

5

Tibidabo

Via Favència

P. de Valldaura

Penitents

P. de Fabra i Puig

P. de la Bonanova

Av. República Argentina

C. de Larrad

Pare Jacinto Alegre

Parc Güell

Av. Mare de Déu de Montserrat

Guinardó

Trav. de Dalt

P. Sant José de la Muntanya

Gràcia

1

Via Augusta

Avenida Princep d'Asturies

Trav. de Gràcia

C. de Sardenya

C. de Marina

Av. de Gaudí

Av. de la Meridiana

C. Gran de Sant Andreu

Plaça
Francesc Macià

12

Av. Diagonal

2

C. Infanta Carlota

C. de Balmes

Rambla de Catalunya

P. de Gràcia

C. de Provença

C. de Aragó

Plaça de les
Glories Catalanes

Av. de Roma

C. de Valencia

11

Plaça
de Tetuán

Carrer de Pere IV

C. de Aragó

Av. Gran Via de les Corts Catalanes

Plaça de
Catalunya

6

F. de Sant Joan

P. de Carles

Sants

Old Town

Plaça de
España

Ramblas

Av. del Paral-lel

C. Nou de la
Rambla

Passeig de Colóm

Barceloneta

4

Av. de Miramar

Muntanya de
Montjuïc

Harbour

Mediterranean

N

Bibliography

It is almost impossible to give an overview of the literature on Antoni Gaudí. Initially, it was only his close friends who commented on his works and intentions. Soon, however, a veritable flood of publications was forthcoming, all concerned with the future-oriented aspects of Gaudí's *oeuvre*.

In 1973, a bibliography compiled by the American Association of Architectural Bibliographers listed 843 publications on Gaudí and his architecture alone.

In the meantime, numerous further texts have been published.

The present book should not be understood as another contribution to research already undertaken on Gaudí; it is supposed to introduce the reader to Gaudí and give him a flavour of Gaudí's work, perhaps encouraging him to travel to Spain (and you do not even have to travel around much, as most buildings can be found in Barcelona).

The select bibliography below is intended to lay the basis for closer reading on Gaudí. The choice hinges on German publications or those relatively easy to obtain in Germany.

A general introduction to Art Nouveau, with a brief series of appraisals of Gaudí's work can be found in:

Madsen, Stefan Tschudi *Jugendstil. Europäische Kunst der Jahrhundertwende*, Munich, 1967;

Schmutzler, Robert *Art Nouveau-Jugendstil*, Stuttgart, 1962.

The comprehensive catalogue produced on the occasion of an exhibition at the Villa Stuck in Munich is to be highly recommended. It is more than just the catalogue of an exhibition, it is a well-illustrated introduction to Gaudí's architecture.

César Martinell's large Gaudí book is invaluable. Martinell spoke with numerous contemporaries of Gaudí and presents comprehensive material on the architect otherwise not available, especially since Gaudí himself hardly ever gave written statements on his work. One therefore has to rely on statements he made in conversation.

Martinell, César *Antoni Gaudí*, (Spanish edition: Barcelona, 1967; Italian ed.: Milan, 1955; English ed.: Barcelona, 1975).

Boeck, Wilhelm Antonio Gaudí. *Katalog einer Ausstellung in Baden-Baden mit knappen Charakterisierungen der Bauten*, Baden-Baden, 1961.

Camprubi-Alemany, F. *Die Kirche der Heiligen Familie in Barcelona*, doctoral thesis, Munich, 1959.

Collins, George R. *Antonio Gaudí*, London, 1960.

Conrads, Ulrich, & Sperlich, Hans G. *Phantastische Architektur*, Stuttgart, 1960.

Dalisi, Riccardo *Antonio Gaudí – Möbel und Objekte*, Stuttgart, 1981.

Giedion-Welcker, C. *Park Güell de A. Gaudí*, Barcelona, 1966 (with texts in Spanish, German, English and French).

Güell, Xavier *Antoni Gaudí*, Zurich and Munich, 1987.

Hitchcock, Henry-Russell *Gaudí*, New York, 1957.

Ràfols, José F. *Gaudí*, Barcelona, 1960 (3rd ed.).

Schweitzer, Albert *Aus meinem Leben und Denken*, Leipzig, 1932 (with reminiscences of Gaudí from early times).

Solà-Morales, Ignasi de *Gaudí*, Stuttgart, 1983.

Sterner, Gabriele *Barcelona: Antoni Gaudí y Corn'et. Architektur als Ereignis*, Cologne, 1979.

Sweeney, James Johnson & Sert, Josep Lluis *Antonio Gaudí*, London, 1970.

Wiedemann, Josef *Antoni Gaudí. Inspiration in Architektur und Handwerk*, Munich, 1974.